THE RESILIENT ENTREPRENEUR
Converting Adversity Into Wealth

eBook: 979-8-9985198-0-2
Paperback: 979-8-9927481-8-5
Hardcover: 979-8-9927481-9-2

Cover design by Sooraj Mathew

The ArtCat .com
CREATIVE SERVICES

Edited by Hilary Jastram, www.bookmarkpub.com

Bookmark
PUBLISHING HOUSE

THE
RESILIENT
ENTREPRENEUR

CONVERTING ADVERSITY
INTO WEALTH

MARC MASON

To my Nana and Grandpa.

For always loving us for exactly who we are.

Get in Touch

www.facebook.com/marcmason2021

www.instagram.com/marcmason_

Table of Contents

Foreword

IMET MARC AT BRISTOL-PLYMOUTH REGIONAL TECHNICAL SCHOOL in 2005, ironically at about the same age he is now when I was teaching plumbing and heating. Marc was a typical teenager, and our relationship now is very different than it was then. Based on early history, I never would have imagined that nearly 20 years later, he would become a close friend. Building long-lasting relationships is usually not typical for students and teachers. I have been fortunate to build many of these relationships through the years, but not all made the dramatic turn this one has.

As I was writing this foreword, I tried to recall Marc's young face and personality. Right off the top of my head, I can picture a youthful Marc always looking for the angle, his mind moving a mile a minute. He wanted to find the advantage to take him out of his trying situation. It was no secret that his home life was a struggle. I mean, his Nana was an angel who always looked closely after Marc, but his parents, to the best of my knowledge, were not part of his life.

At the time, cell phones were just gaining traction, and Marc used that to try and get ahead, selling ringtones and repairing phones and flipping them to classmates. Marc wanted to know all about whatever was on the technological horizon, so he could use it to his benefit. He would take every opportunity to get ahead. I even recall an incident where he sold my Mountain Dew to his classmates. The kids always looked up to him, although, by his own admission, he was not a very good student. That's not why they admired him. I think they could see something deeper was at play in Marc. They could see his potential, too, like I could. But I didn't notice it right away. Marc would make me wait a few years until he showed that part of himself. He initially struggled in the classroom but was pretty good in the shop.

I'll never forget Marc's sophomore year. He was very close to getting expelled, having a hard time focusing on his work, and getting into trouble. My partner and I reeled him in and had a tough love conversation with him. We had to lay it on the line, and something must've shifted in him from that talk because, from that point on, I saw him refocus on what he needed to do and a new belief take root that he could use the skills from Bristol-Plymouth to create a prosperous career for himself. But even as he applied what he learned, I don't think he ever dreamed that he could achieve the goals and accomplishments that he has today. His self-confidence evolved to the point that he knew whatever he put his mind to, he could attain.

Since our childhoods were similar, Marc and I connected on a personal level. He was living with his grandmother when he was in high school, and for a good portion of my life, I was also raised by my grandmother and had struggles at home. I graduated and went to college for a year but could not afford the tuition, so I joined the military. While in the service, I got married and eventually moved back home, falling back on the skills I learned when I went to vocational school. I worked hard and excelled fast. I eventually concluded that I should be self-employed and started my own business. Early on, I was struggling to find good help and found myself building a new plumbing program at Bristol-Plymouth while simultaneously running the business. This is where I met Marc—amid keeping the business afloat and developing a brand-new plumbing program for the school.

Marc's life was very familiar to me. I sympathized with his feelings of not knowing the next step to leave his old life behind, and I wanted to help him reach his goals. Marc tells me that he gravitated toward me because of my military background. His grandfather, who you'll learn about shortly, was also a military man. When Marc lost him prematurely, I think he saw me as a sort of substitution for the missing father figure in his life. At first, Marc didn't like me. I know I'm tough on the kids sometimes, but I'm also fair. I didn't and still don't put up with any bullshit and held the students accountable. It wasn't until senior year when I was helping Marc with his senior project, that he started to change his tune. I could see how motivated and positive he was becoming and that he was finally appreciating his potential return on investment.

After he graduated, Marc and I stayed close, and I helped him prepare for his licensing exam. He would be the first licensed plumber that Bristol-Plymouth turned out and then the first master plumber. His hard work during his senior year of high school earned him a job at Sagamore Plumbing & Heating, where he quickly excelled out in the field. Then, one day, he slipped and fell, tearing his meniscus, so he was reassigned to the office, which was actually a good turn of events. It helped him fast-track his path into estimating and project management. While that was going on, he was hustling and buying properties, continually putting himself out there.

Marc just kept working and overextending himself. He took many risks, and it all paid off, not because he was lucky but because he willed it to happen. Watching him use what was at his disposal and turn it into something amazing was incredibly inspiring.

I would tell my incoming students, as well as my own children, "There's a local kid who graduated from this program. He put his mind to it, and now, he's achieving great things." Without fully disclosing his net worth, I would tell the kids Marc was going to be a millionaire someday. I hoped telling them all about his successes and the properties he was buying and fixing would help motivate them and demonstrate the opportunities they could take advantage of. As the years went on, it was cool when the kids would shout out his name to me when I was telling his story. This proved he was making a difference and honestly made me feel like I was, too. Marc was still living with his grandmother then, but that didn't stop him from going after what he dreamed of and being smart with his money. This was when he started buying rental properties, and boy, was he frugal. We'd get together; he'd tell me how many units he'd acquired and that he wasn't touching his regular employment salary. It was going right into the bank. Unlike other kids who had found early success coming out of the program, Marc didn't have a new vehicle or anything obvious that demonstrated he was winning. He refused to waste his money and was constantly reinvesting it. It was a lot of hard work, but he stayed focused. His diligence was admirable.

I'm sure as Marc was building this foundation for his new life, that people were jealous of what he was doing. Those in his circle really didn't understand his focus and drive. Still, he didn't let that bother or stop him. He was determined to do everything he could to change his circumstances. And in some instances, he even changed the people around him. He talks about that with you here, how sometimes, we need to take a look around at the company we keep and determine if anyone is holding us back. If that's the case, there's one thing to do: what's best for you. You can't succeed among people who don't want you to. You'll compete with their voices tearing you down. If you don't know how to make this change, Marc gives you his best advice a little later on. Always choose yourself.

It wasn't enough for Marc to work on improving his own life. He began paying it forward and helping the community. He's done a tremendous amount for the city of Taunton, taking old, rundown properties and renovating them into homes for people who really needed them in the middle of the housing crisis. That's the mindset of a leader, someone who thinks outside of themselves, someone who wants to make everything and everyone around them better.

I'm extremely proud to have had Marc as a student and even prouder to call him a close friend. I appreciate everything he's done for the local community and what he continues to do for his employees at RCL Mechanical, another business built from the ground up that he co-owns and that he operated while working in real estate development and property investment and management.

Marc's book covers what I've told students for 25-30 years, including my own children: If you want to get anywhere and change your life, keep a positive attitude and stay consistent with your goals. You must concentrate on what you can control and let go of what you can't.

Some people get stuck in a rut, and if this is you, it doesn't mean you can't get out of it. You don't want to be one of those who stay rooted in one place. They can't shift their lives because, to them, everything's going wrong around them. Their circumstances compound, and they consistently make bad decisions. Knowing how people stay in one place is the first part of the equation. The second is ensuring you make better decisions, so you don't find yourself there. Marc could've condemned himself to a lifetime of more suffering; he could have felt sorry for himself and allowed it to swallow him up until there was nothing left but hopelessness, but he chose to rise above the hand of cards he was dealt—which he'll talk about as it pertains to your life. We're all dealt a hand of cards. Some people have better hands than others. But, as Marc will tell you, that doesn't matter. All that matters is the fight in you.

Marc's always been a fighter, and through his words, he is trying to instill that quality in you. Things didn't come easy for him, but he is a person who wants to know how to be better. To this day, I still privately correct him on social media when he makes the occasional mistake, and he doesn't dwell on it or permit it to make him feel negative or wrong. He fights through any thoughts that might come up to potentially sabotage him. He wants the constructive criticism to be better. He would never let himself be the driver, deliberately derailing himself. No matter the context, Marc will make the sacrifice that you have to make as an entrepreneur to earn success. He's not afraid to fall and pick himself back up.

Maybe you know this already, but there's no easy path to success. It takes vision—which Marc talks about at length in the coming pages. You need to understand and project what your dreams can and will look like . . . and you will hear this next part a lot . . . you must take the high road when it comes to your thoughts.

There's no negativity with Marc. It just doesn't exist. That's what I love about him. No matter what you throw at him, he is solutions-driven. He'll find a way regardless of the level of hard work it entails. I subscribe to the same mindset. When people come to me with problems, I always focus on solutions. I model resilience—yet another topic Marc is covering in this book.

I'm thrilled that Marc wrote this book to share his thoughts with the world to help the people who need a little push to get out of their own way. He's crafted this book in a unique way, detailing his life events and lessons that he's applied to his life even today, like honing your vision, learning resilience, applying gratitude when life is really kicking the hell out of you, and so much more. Marc then talks about taking these principles and using them to build a long-lasting business. He teaches you all about developing a business plan, mission statement, core values, and even marketing when you get far enough along to need to implement it. It doesn't matter where you are in your life or what adversities you are facing. You can get ahead. You can make a change. You can do anything you dream of. All you have to do is start with the belief in yourself and then keep at it like Marc is . . . Being positive means conditioning your brain every day to think about the advantages at your disposal—and that includes applying knowledge learned from the darkest times in your life. You need that knowledge and the subsequent skillsets if you are going to move forward.

The old saying goes that knowledge is useless unless you use it. Make sure you take what Marc is teaching you to help construct the life of your dreams. Turn to this book again and again on the different pathways in your journey. You can use it through any step of the process. Although we have never had the pleasure of meeting, Marc and I both believe that you can do what you put your mind to. But that doesn't matter. The only thing that does is that you believe in yourself.

To your success!

Rick McGrath
Tradesman/ Educator/ Mentor

Introduction

"FUCK YOU, asshole!"

Not exactly words you typically hear out of the mouth of a baby learning to talk but that was me, and it's the perfect way to begin my story.

If you ask any member of my family to describe me when I was little, they will undoubtedly have a lot to say, and honestly, it will likely be a version of how bad I was . . . but usually, me swearing like a sailor before I was two years old will be brought up for sure.

Why is this important to my story of success? Because we have to know where we have been to understand where we are. Now, if I run into someone while I'm out and about and they knew me as a kid, without fail, they will make mention that I should be proud of where I am because with my circumstances growing up, it would have been easy for me to end up down a bad path.

1

I always say, "Life is a journey, not a destination . . ." And my journey has had many bumps and rough terrain to get me where I am today.

What is Normal?

My family has never looked "normal" or "traditional." They were blended before I was even born, before my mother was even born, and being that my grandparents were each other's second spouses, they had seven children between them when they got married, and then they had my mother together.

My mother got pregnant with my older brother when she was 17 years old, and about three years later, I came along. He and I have different fathers. But where he knew who his father was, I never did. We also had a baby sister, Mary. Not many people know about Mary. That's because she never got to live but mere moments out of the womb. She died not long after she was born due to my mother's drug use while she was pregnant with her.

I don't remember very much about my mother because when I was nine years old, she died of a drug overdose, but that isn't what my brother and I were told. We were just told she was sick. And in many ways, she was.

It wasn't until many years later that I learned the truth. But the fact of the matter is that even before she died, I knew that my brother and I were growing up differently than everyone else.

I remember my mother being strict when I was really young, but over time, she began paying less attention to us. I think now that must have been when she started to get more and more into drugs. I remember her bringing different men around, and my brother and I were often left to fend for ourselves. We were quite young since we went to live with my grandparents, my Nana and Grandpa, permanently when I was four.

My earliest memory is me in my old house, which I lived in with my mother and my brother, the memory of an unsettling home with writing all over the bedroom walls and always being nervous about people coming in and out at all hours of the day and night, sometimes through my brother's and my bedroom window. One time, they even broke the window coming in, and there was glass all over our room. I remember people looking in our windows and never feeling fully safe. I was once asked to describe my childhood before moving in with my grandparents in one word, and the only word that I could really think of was "neglected."

If I had to really think back, I can vaguely remember my mother being strict with my brother and me in a more parental way as opposed to an irritable addict way. It was actually a pretty stark contrast to how she ended up becoming. She was very much a "Do as I say, not as I do" parent.

Remember how I said I swore like a sailor . . . ? Well, where do you think I learned that language?

She and the people she used to bring around taught me. But heaven help me if I swore in front of her when we were little because she would actually wash our mouths out with soap, or we would get a whooping.

She was also particularly strict about certain things; like we had to eat all our supper before we could get a drink. Which was sometimes a task because we were on government assistance and the amount of frozen fish sticks I had to consume . . . Let's just say that my brother and I will be happy if we never see a fish stick again in our lives.

Even though I remember her being strict with us about those things, when I was younger, I used to miss this behavior because at least she was paying attention to what we were doing and, in her own way, caring about us getting the food that we needed. As she got more and more into drugs, it was just a blur of neglect and her getting angry at us for no reason.

Even during the time that my mother had custody of us and we lived with her, we would often stay with our grandparents. They were always our safe haven. We preferred to be there rather than at the house we shared with our mother. So much so that when we were misbehaving while at Nana and Grandpa's (which we often were), Nana would say, "If you don't stop it, I am going to send you back to . . ." and she would name our mother's address. You better believe we would change our behavior because that address was in an unsavory neighborhood with unsavory people, and as I said before . . . they were the people going through the revolving door in and out of our "home."

As much of a safe place as our grandparent's home was, we couldn't always be there. But there is one person who has always been my safe place. One person who I always knew wouldn't let anything happen to me if he could help it. He was my hope. That person is my big brother. My brother always made me feel safe even if things were off and unsteady in our world. He would always give me the sense that everything would be okay. My brother has been my protector all of my life, and considering he is only three years older than me, that was a lot for a child to take on. What choice did either of us really have? We learned survival at a very young age.

When my mother got deeper into drugs, the environment became very unsafe for us. It wasn't uncommon to be kept up at night because the "adults" were partying and to see those same "adults" nodding off at random hours of the day and night or finding used needles and dried-up blood in our apartment. These were things that I lived with at a very young age. Needless to say, we were removed from that home and her custody.

We were finally living in a safe environment at Nana and Grandpa's house, but that didn't mean that the long reach of my mother's continued addiction still didn't touch and impact our lives. I think she had good intentions of trying to get sober, and when she was visiting when we lived at Nana's, she would bring gifts when she came—which wasn't a lot, but she would try her best. She always used to doze off when she was over, and I remember thinking she was really tired—until I got older and realized why she was "tired."

Once we were taken from her, she struggled even more and ended up in jail a few times. Recently, my brother, Scott, and I were going through pictures, and we came across one of the three of us: my brother, my mother, and me. My mom was almost unrecognizable to me. Fucking drugs . . . She died not long after that photo was taken.

Don't get me wrong. I loved my mother, but it is a complicated kind of love. A love that takes time to understand and work through. Children give unconditional love, and my brother and I were no different. We loved our mother. And despite all that we experienced and went through with her, and because of her, we still cherish her and her memory in many ways. It's complicated. The thing is . . .

when you are living a life like I was, it's hard to understand how someone who was meant to take care of you, to protect you, and to love you could let you live and be treated the way we were when we were in her care. So, I did what a lot of children do, I coped.

How did I cope? To put it plainly, I acted out. I became a problem in many ways and to many people.

Honestly, a lot of those behaviors I mutated to my benefit, and they helped catapult me into success throughout my life.

The world throws us curveballs all the time, and it sometimes feels like the beginning of my life was all curveballs. It was a game of survival in many ways. Living in this environment fundamentally impacted my brother and me in a way that is hard to describe.

For a long time, I didn't even acknowledge that part of my life, and honestly, I sometimes struggle to pull those memories out because my brain locked them away so I wouldn't have to relive them. Sharing this with anyone, much less the world, is not easy by any means, but it is necessary to share. We all have choices to make, and often, that looks like people leaning in/giving in to their circumstances. OR you can choose to overcome and be different. Even at a young age, the life I was living unsettled me, and I rebelled against it in so many ways. That has looked different through the years, but ultimately, it has led me to the success that I have today.

What Cards Are You Holding?

I often say, "Not everyone's dealt the same cards."

It's a saying we've heard many times, but what does it really mean?

As a concept, it seems pretty unfair that some people have to strive harder to get past more pain and obstacles than others. But that's the truth. If you can relate, maybe it will make you feel better to know I can, too.

I've lived and breathed this just like you may have, but when I stopped obsessing about it, my life changed.

The truth is that everyone has a different past—everyone has a unique set of different cards. Everyone grows up differently. Everyone has tragedies. These are the cards we are dealt.

They are not necessarily bad cards. They just are our cards. In some cases, they are also our adversities.

Utilize this book as your tool to navigate through your adversities, extract the strengths, and acknowledge the weaknesses in order to come out on the other side. This is precisely what I did when confronted with the many roads I could have taken. Since then, I have changed my life to make it the one I dreamed of. I have every confidence that you can do this, too.

Getting over and Accepting Adversity

First, I want you to know that there are many ways to conquer your adversities.

Before considering the options you can take, give yourself permission to accept who you are and the hand you have been dealt. Use that as fire to reach your dreams! This is your hidden strength, and you can put it to work for you.

I want you to focus on your hidden strengths because many people focus on their weaknesses rather than magnifying their strengths. It can be hard to do this if you don't know how.

Sometimes, all we need is a little introspection to find the answer we have been looking for. I encourage you to take an hour and determine how you've gotten stronger because of what you've gone through. Listen to your mind, soul, and gut. Let it tell you on a subconscious level what you already know. When you tap into your intuition, you will not go wrong.

Although years have gone by, I remember wanting a different life. Mostly, I thought about the family aspect. Everyone else's parents were together at school. All the other kids had toys to play with, like brand-new four-wheelers. I wanted what everyone else could afford. All the conversations we had as a kid were: "We don't have the money for that," or "Money's tight." We were in shambles, but I was grateful even as I longed to put together a family with the correct elements when I was older, so I could finally do what I wanted with them.

When I talk about honoring and trusting the path you're on and being the best YOU can be, I'm talking to myself, too. I still have to remind myself that I know what is best and that I am capable of getting to the levels I want. You are, too. Be confident and defeat what is known as imposter syndrome.

Learning to trust and honor yourself is not easy. It takes consistent work to choose yourself and respect your unique path that will always have bumps in the road. That's just a fact of life, and the sooner we can accept that, the better off we will be.

Life is a series of forward movements despite our hardships. There is no destination or finish line. It is really about the continuous journey that fills your cup to create your happiness. Remember to be grateful for where you are and how far you have come. We tend to always look back at the negative, which makes it hard to look forward. When you focus on the positive, you will attract positive changes. This is the mindset shift you need to achieve the future you desire.

I advise you to work quickly because time is of the essence. The average person lives to be 85 years old, and it goes fast.

How old are you?

How many more summers do you think you have left if you live to the average age?

Don't you want to live your life to your potential?

What does that look like? What are your dreams?

Just like we all have different pasts, we all have different goals. Do you want to create a legacy? Do you want to be the ONE who changes the trajectory for your family? You may even give them the blueprint to follow in your footsteps.

My hope is to be able to do that for my family, especially my daughter. I want to be able to guide her and be a role model she can look up to. I want her to learn valuable traits by observing me. I aspire to be the positive example I never had growing up, providing her with the support and guidance I lacked. I want to cultivate an environment where she feels inspired and learns from my actions, ensuring she grows up with the strong foundation and mentorship that every child deserves.

There is no better feeling than having the opportunity to help someone. I call this "reaching down to help someone up," and it's one of my favorite things to do. I love it when people reach out and ask me for advice, whether about business, real estate, or life in general. I have had many mentors, coaches, and people in my life who have helped me when I needed it. Looking back, I did not always deserve some of the help that I was given. Like I said at the beginning of the book, I was rough around the edges. I am thankful for the people who looked past some of my "flaws" and saw potential in me.

One of those people was Rick McGrath, the writer of this book's foreword. Rick was my vocational high school plumbing teacher, and we have a relationship today dating back from all those years ago. He was an inspiration, and I looked up to him so much when I was in school. Rick motivated me and got me ready for success, especially when I was working on my senior project. His military style reminded me of my grandfather, who was a veteran. Rick encouraged me so much that I became the first licensed master plumber to graduate from that school.

I am asking you all these questions about what you want for your life because I am *the one* who is changing it in my family, and there is no better feeling than that.

The Gift of Being Self-Aware

As you move past your adversity, you must constantly be self-aware. Self-awareness is an ever-changing compilation of discipline and resilience.

Remember, as you are striving to make these positive changes in your life you are not perfect. Let me speak for myself when I say that I am far from perfect. If you get off track or lost, it's okay. You can learn to control and train your mind to overcome self-limiting thoughts and beliefs. It's imperative that you condition yourself to bounce back from disappointments. In life, failures will arise; however, this can lead to growth as an individual.

I can vividly remember having to choose a high school. I had my heart set on a vocational school, but acceptance wasn't guaranteed. My grades and behavior didn't exactly help my case, and I wasn't initially accepted. I was frustrated at the thought of having to attend a different school but knew I'd be okay if that were the case; it just wouldn't be my first choice. Enter my older brother Scott. He attended the vocational high school and was the master string-puller. Thanks to him, I got in. Thanks, Scott, for always having my back! If I hadn't attended that vocational school, I can guarantee that I would not be where I am today. The school taught me a trade, I met some incredible teachers, and with a lot of hard work, routine, and ambition, I was able to start my own company. I was given the fundamentals I needed to get on my feet once I graduated from high school while also making good money.

However, it was a rocky start for me. I was young when I graduated from high school and still had a lot of growing up to do and lessons to learn. I believe that life happens for you, not to you.

Let me just remind you that it took a lot of lessons and growth to get where I am today. When I was applying for jobs after I graduated from high school, I applied to MCI Plymouth as a maintenance plumber. Not only did I not get the job, but I didn't even make it to the interview . . . Life Lesson 101—Don't go out and drink the night before with your friends; it does not always end well. That night, I drank too much, and a friend and I decided it was a good idea to give a lawn job to some poor, innocent person. Looking back, I do not know what I was thinking, but let's just say I paid for that poor choice and got arrested. That's why I missed my interview. I was not meant to get that job. The universe had different plans for me.

At my vocational school, I had many great teachers over the years, but Rick was a role model and someone I felt that I could always count on. Unlike a lot of people in my life, he was one of the few who saw potential in me.

When I was searching for a job and then did not get the job at MCI due to my "mishap," this teacher gave me a recommendation to a well-known plumbing company that was hiring. I got a job as an apprentice plumber and worked there for 10 years. I worked my way up to a management role. I loved my job but knew that I wanted to create my own legacy. It's not easy to step out of your comfort zone, and that is why it took me as long as it did before I decided to leave my steady job and start my own business. It was the scariest but best decision I ever could have made.

That's why you need this book and all the tools within to transform your mindset—they are the very ones I used with my own. As soon as I reached a significant change where I knew I would never go back, I wanted to help other people do the same.

Resist Comparing Yourself on Your Way Up

If you can resist comparing yourself to other people, no matter the context, you're winning. The reality is it's you versus you. Our society and the ever-increasing visibility of people on social media make it easy to measure yourself against your friends, family, and influences. But make no mistake; we are seeing someone else's highlight reel, so we cannot compare the realities of our lives—which includes our struggles with them.

As a kid, I can remember wishing that I had more than what I had. I found myself envious of others at times. I had friends who went on vacations, had snowmobiles, and were always doing fun things on the weekends. Like any kid, you want what everyone else has. However, as I grow older, I realize that having to work hard to get the things I want/need is my fuel and a gratifying feeling.

Think about your dreams and the stories within them. All dreams have a backstory of what it was really like behind the scenes or before things improved.

What story are you holding deep inside that you are afraid to let out? What embarrasses you? What do you need to face that you don't think anyone else has gone through?

I'm not suggesting that you make a big, intimidating announcement to the world. Simply let out your thoughts and feelings to someone else about what you think is holding you back. Talk to a person you trust and get it out. You can't carry around pain and trauma for the rest of your life. Releasing and working through it is a huge part of moving forward. When starting this book, I spoke with family members about memories from my childhood that I had suppressed. It was a scary but healing process.

Talking about my past and family was not something that I did. I was the prime example of someone who "bottled up" my emotions. I never wanted anyone to feel bad or sorry for me, and I did not want to open up old wounds. As I got older, I realized that I had trained myself to forget a lot of the awful things that I went through. I repressed a lot of my memories involving trauma as a defense mechanism. I recently learned that when you repress things, it involves unconsciously blocking out distressing thoughts, memories, or feelings from conscious awareness to protect oneself. I have worked very hard over the years to try and process my past. I am a firm believer in working on yourself physically, mentally, and emotionally.

I have worked with different coaches and mentors, and I am a part of a handful of groups that have like-minded individuals who I now feel comfortable confiding in. From all of this "self-work" I feel more myself than I ever have.

As you strive for your aims, life will give you detours, but stay the course. Some might have to do with the shame you're carrying or your lack of self-esteem. Decide which road you will take and what you will retain or release and why. It doesn't hurt to put a little pressure on yourself to deflect distractions like overwhelming emotions and shiny-object syndrome, either. Keep at the front of your mind that everyone is counting on you. You simply can't stay where you are—not if you intend to be the example to pave the way not just for yourself but for others who need it and may follow in your footsteps.

If you do have a problem with giving yourself credit, look at the small wins rather than the losses. Failures and losses are a needed evil to succeed. If you consistently win, you have no gain. What takes you to the next level are adversity and obstacles.

It's Time to Accept and Love Yourself

I wrote this book for several reasons; one is that I NEED you to accept and love who you are and where you are in life right now. That's easier said than done, I know, and you will need to work at it to make it a part of your daily routine. Remember, we are simply born into some of the adversities we have to overcome, so there is no reason to come down on yourself for something you cannot control.

When I used to feel caught in the trauma of my past, I would stop and think about what I am grateful for. This is a guaranteed way to shift the direction of your emotions. Ask any of my friends; I am forever saying to them, "What are you grateful for today?" I will instill this practice with my daughter, too. Everyone should practice this daily.

My mentor introduced me to practicing daily gratitude, and I continue to do so to this day. Remembering to be grateful also made me realize I need to be more conscious of identifying my blessings. There are some days when I don't stop all day, and it can be easy not to do little things because I am caught up with work, our family, or life in general. But I try to take a few minutes to think of at least one thing I am grateful for daily.

When you value what you have, it untaps a superpower that will truly help you. Today, agree you will not fall victim to your past. Let it point you in the right direction of your future. Give thanks for the lessons you have learned that have made you stronger, then use a few of these actions to move ahead:

1. Write down what you're struggling to let go.
2. Learn to forgive.
3. Commit to self-education.
4. Celebrate little and big wins.

The second you cracked open this book, you made a pledge to change your life for the better. Now, you can train your mind to hold to your promises and get comfortable being uncomfortable. These are big, sweeping changes you are embarking on making. Some days, you will want to quit because striking out on your own is so hard; that's normal. But you know you can't afford to do that. So, make the choice now before we even get started. Can you handle the hard?

I know you can. Do you know that? If you are feeling unsure, flip back a couple of pages and read the part about strength and how your trials have given you the tools you need to develop the life you want.

If you have to fight to get out from under circumstances beyond your control, like I did, you're forged from tough stuff.

What will make you tougher is wanting your dreams more than your struggles. Use this fact to propel you to the greatest heights beyond what you can't even imagine.

Right now, struggle is what you know. I want to share with you what you don't know and the secrets that will get you ahead to get you anything you desire in life.

Your first step is simple.

Just turn the page.

1

My Cards

"Opportunities don't happen. You create them."

−*Chris Grosser*

My Cards

I'LL USE THE CARDS I WAS DEALT as proof that you can conquer even the deepest demons. Before I started reclaiming my life, if you looked at me on paper, I wouldn't have had a chance—no matter what area of life we're talking about: job prospects, finances, growth, it didn't matter. I was born behind the eight ball.

Are you feeling this way, buried under the weight of where you were born, your upbringing, poverty, or anything else designed to keep you down? So many people start out this way. It can make you feel disconnected from the person who has gotten out or overcome what was trying to hold them back.

It's true. I look great on paper now, but don't look at where I am and think you have such a long way to go. Take into account where I came from—a place very similar to where you may be now—then map out your circumstances one step at a time–like I did.

But I don't want to get ahead of myself. When your life is so turned around that you don't know what step to take or where to go, it can be intimidating. Or maybe you feel like every choice you have made in the past was the wrong one. It can be hard to trust yourself when you feel like you are failing.

Then there's the "American Dream" and the idea that we should all be shooting for achieving certain goals. That can feel like a longshot when you don't have resources or the information you need to make meaningful changes.

Once you give yourself permission to dream and figure out your next step, remember that the "American Dream" looks different for everyone. There is no right or wrong answer for reaching this dream because there isn't a perfect one-size-fits-all life. You have to find what feels right for you. You have to figure out how to get from one point to another, and no one else will do it for you.

This is all complicated by well-meaning people.

Did you hear this kind of advice growing up?

"After high school, you have to apply for college."

"You need a degree. No one in our family has graduated high school, so you must."

This kind of advice from people who don't understand that life paths aren't uniform can make things worse and cause added pressure.

It can be hard to know what you want, especially when everyone is giving you advice. It can be tempting to want to do what everyone else is doing. I felt pressure at times to apply and go to college. But again, I was young and didn't have a clue about what I wanted to do for the rest of my life. I knew no matter what I decided that working would have to be part of my plan. If I ended up going to college, I would have to make money to pay my tuition and bills, support my lifestyle, and save money for the future. I never had anyone financially support me. My Nana did her best, but she did not have much to offer in this way. My brother and I were also trying to help her with her bills.

I remember going with one of my friends and talking to someone about attending Bristol Community College, but after weighing out the pros and cons, I decided it wasn't for me. At the time, it made sense to use the trade I'd learned, plumbing, and go into the field and start working. I started out making good money, and I liked what I was doing.

I like challenges, and when I have my mind set on something, I make it happen. I have always been that way. I started out at the bottom and worked my way up. I never envisioned myself being an "office guy," but I got hurt while working in the field and ended up doing estimates for jobs and then became a project manager. I didn't think that I was going to like it, but I ended up loving it. That's when I started to realize I was meant to be a leader and manage people. I also know what I want by now. If you don't, I urge you to figure that out. Ask yourself, *what drives me?* I am where I belong because I have an opportunity to lead, train, and mentor others in the field. It's very natural to me.

A Rough Start

Let's go back to when I was young and how my life started. I talked about this at the beginning of the book, but there is a lot more that I want to share with you. Sometimes, when I think back on my life, I am amazed that I was able to create the life that I have now.

Before I moved into my grandparents' home, my baby bottle was filled with sugary drinks, from Kool-Aid to Pepsi. If I were still practicing those horrible habits from my childhood, I probably wouldn't have any teeth! When I woke up and figured out I had to leave bad habits behind, I promised myself I would be a different kind of adult. Sometimes, it's as easy as saying to yourself, *I know this isn't right for me, so I'm not going to do it!* Sometimes, you might need to rehearse what you will say to the person pressuring you so you can stand your ground.

Maybe you weren't taught the right morals or ethics. Maybe you didn't grow up in a wealthy household. That was my case, and I know now that it doesn't matter where you came from. You can build from your current foundation using what you know.

Whatever you do, though, do not allow it to hold you back; use it to get ahead.

I didn't go to college; I was a C student, and nothing came easy to me. I was dealt the worst hand in the deck, but I wanted so much more that, ultimately, my cards didn't matter. I turned those cards into a royal flush and changed my trajectory for good. At a young age, I learned a lot of survival skills that have helped me get where I am today, along with the unconditional love and support from family and friends.

Safe but Not Sound

To put it plainly, Nana and Grandpa were my everything. My saviors. My safe place. My parents. Now, I would like to tell you that because they were all of this to me, I was an angel to them. I really fucking wasn't, though; I was quite the little shit, and I put my grandparents through a lot. To their credit, they never gave up on me and always believed in me. Although if you ask most people, they will say that my Nana just let me get away with everything . . . I mean, they might be right, but who cares? Not me. She was a walking angel. My grandpa though, he didn't let any of us get away with anything. Nana and Grandpa were polar opposites.

Living at Nana and Grandpa's always made me feel wanted and safe, but that didn't mean my experiences didn't follow me into that safe space. I was plagued with nightmares. Every night. So, I slept with my Nana and Grandpa every night, and when I got a bit older, they had a couch in their room specifically for me to sleep on. It didn't always keep the nightmares away, but they always comforted me when they would wake me up. They were a living reminder that I was safe and wanted—that I wasn't back there. They were the consistency that I needed in my life.

It wasn't just the nightmares. When you live in chaos and an environment without guidance, you become feral in many ways; at least, I did. When I tell you that I straight-up refused to get on the school bus to go to Head Start, I mean I threw down the tantrum of all tantrums, which usually included my grandpa having to try and wrestle me on the bus and ultimately resulted in him driving me there himself and basically dragging me into my classroom. Gotta give that man credit, he didn't have patience for a lot of things, but he would always get my ass to school.

What would I do once I was there, you ask? I would hide under the table and refuse to do what they told me to. I'll tell you this: being my teacher wasn't a job for the faint of heart. I was defiant and wanted to do what I wanted at all times.

I eventually grew out of doing those things, but that didn't mean I grew out of pressing buttons and thinking of school rules and policies more like guidelines I didn't have to follow. But those are stories for a little bit later on.

One of the ways that I got beyond the tantrums was the structure and consistency living with my grandparents provided. And Grandpa was structure personified. Where my Nana generally let me get away with everything, Grandpa never let me get away with anything. Grandpa was, and still is, one of the major role models in my life because he gave me a sense of purpose and fulfillment along with structure. He taught me that tough love shapes a strong, disciplined man, that the little lessons and memories shape a man to be who they become at a young age.

Grandpa was an engineer and a proud Marine veteran of the Korean War. Maybe it was his history as a Marine that made him so strict, but I will tell you what. That man didn't play around. On Saturday mornings, at the crack of dawn, my brother and I would be woken up at 6:00 a.m. by "Reveille." If you're not familiar, it's the trumpet going . . . "Doot, Doot, Do-Da, Doot, Doot, Doot, Do-Da, Doot, Doot, Doot, Do-Da, Doot, Dooo, Dooo . . ." And we would be expected to be up and out of bed ready to work. Did I mention that there was a giant field behind my grandparent's house? It was up to us

to cut that field. When I say it took hours . . . I mean h o u
r s. Complaining was not tolerated. That was just one chore
we were expected to attend to. But Grandpa would pay us in
ice cream or soda, usually Sam's Choice Caffeine-Free Diet
Cola . . . eventually, we worked our way up to an allowance
and paintball ammo.

The Short Version: My Living Nightmare

I have encountered many tragic situations in my life,
especially as a child, but this one takes the cake. To this day,
I can remember every detail of this day, down the weather,
what I was wearing, and who was there.

My grandfather was outside with my brother and my best
friend, who was my neighbor, and we were all playing and
enjoying the day when some punk in our neighborhood
decided to make a scene and got into an altercation with my
grandfather. My grandfather was a man who tried to instill
values and was not one to let someone disrespect him, so he
went to go cross the street, and BOOM . . . he was struck by a
car and instantly passed right in front of my very own eyes.

The world lost the best man that day. A piece of me died
that day, too. I needed him, and he was taken from me
far too soon. I felt like everyone was leaving me. My world
continued to turn on me. He was the one father figure I had,
and just like that, he was gone. A little altercation with a
neighborhood kid and my life flipped.

*The short period I spent with my grandfather raising me was the
most impactful of my childhood. This is where I get my "gas," as I
put it, to keep going and push myself to the furthest reaches of my
imagination.*

Do you have a grandfather or a father figure? I called mine Grandpa. Maybe you call yours Papa?

When Grandpa was ripped cruelly from this world, I was lost, angry, sad, and a whirl of unpredictable emotions. We all have low moments in life. This was one of my lowest. The point is to find a way to move past these times. I kept asking myself, *why do all these awful things keep happening to me? How is any of this fair?* I felt like my world was falling apart as I fought these demons—my thoughts running away from me. I was scared all the time and had nightmares every night. As an adult, I understand why this was the case, but as a kid, it was so hard. Thankfully, I have worked diligently to train my mindset to use healthier coping skills.

I remember feeling maybe as low as you do right now. This is why I'm talking to you. I want YOU to know what's possible.

Life went on like it does. I attended middle and high school, lost and trying to find myself. During these years, I was not my best self. Looking back, I learned a lot of lessons the hard way and got into a lot of trouble. Now, I can see that the tween and teen years are the most important, as this is where a vast percentage of young people take the wrong path. I was teetering on the edge of that path, keeping company with people doing the wrong things.

Now, I am 33 years old, writing a book with a one-year-old daughter, Demi, and an amazing, supportive wife, Jenna. We live in a beautiful home that I built. I have not one but two 8-figure businesses with 100 employees and over $20 million in revenue between both.

I found my purpose after reflecting on it in a way I am teaching you to do. I look for opportunities and leadership potential in all areas of my life.

I don't share these details to impress you; I want to impress them upon you. I did not inherit money or have handouts. I didn't even begin at ground zero, as you now know. I was entombed in challenges. I had to tunnel my way up, clawing and scratching just to gain a grip.

I'll say it again, and I'll say it often: If I can do this, so can you. Have you ever heard the saying, "If you think it, you can have it?"

Manifest who you want to be. I just dropped a lot on you, so let's talk about you and what your life can look like after you read this book. Close your eyes, and look down. What kind of clothes are you wearing? What is your body type? Now, take the time to write down the steps needed to make desired changes in these areas. Not enough people take the time to sit and get intentional about where they want to go. Today, life moves so fast, and everything is on the fly. Pause to get familiar with what you want to be and do.

Overcoming the Past

It might sound like a less obvious way to make progress, but the way to overcome adversities and hardships is to talk about them. This is why I'm sharing my personal hardships throughout this book. It's challenging to relive that pain. But I was never one to fold under a challenge. If I want to truly give value and change at least ONE person's life, I have to do the hard stuff.

I have to go first.

My mother, Evelynn, had an addiction to drugs—and even though I was very young and couldn't put into words what was wrong, I knew something was. My older brother Scott and I went to live with my grandparents when we were so little because it was getting so bad at my mother's apartment. My grandparents wanted my mother to make better choices so that they didn't have to step in and intervene, but it was bad. If they didn't, it was only a matter of time before we would be taken by DCF or something would have happened to us. When I stop and think about how we were living, it breaks my heart for several reasons: it was a scary place, and no kid should live in the conditions I was living in.

My few memories of my mother include her being absent. How can it be that I remember her if she was gone? Because even when she was around, she was still not present, as she was unfortunately addicted to heroin and had her own battles. I believe she was a fighter and wanted to regain custody of her two children—to give this mothering thing another shot. Unfortunately, she could not overcome her bad hand and walked the wrong path. The upsetting part was that she was only 22 years old—but still old enough to know right from wrong.

You never know what someone is going through. This is why we must forgive and use our cards as leverage to fuel our lives versus falling victim to someone else's "why." A saying I heard once that might make this concept clearer is something along the lines of "If you don't know your 'why,' you will become a part of someone else's."

Live your life deliberately. Choose the experiences you want and what impact you want to make.

Grandpa

Red Mason, or as I know him best, Grandpa, was a husband, father, grandfather, US Marine, and leader. As I sit back and think about our short time together, I remember him providing me with the vision, work ethic, and discipline for the basics of life. He was an amazing man, and I am very blessed to have had him in my life, even though it was shorter than I would have liked. I see a lot of myself in him.

He was very tough on my brother and me, but it was only because he loved us and wanted to teach us right from wrong and how to be a strong man with good morals, as he knew we were not learning those things with our mother and the people she was surrounding us with. He was the definition of tough love. He knew my brother Scott and I had a lot of potential and wanted to see us succeed in life. I think it broke his heart to watch us have to go through everything we did at such a young age. He tried to shield us as much as he could but only had so much control over how my mother was raising us.

Grandpa saw our potential and that we weren't getting the love and support we needed from our mother. He wanted to give us all the tools and resources to reach it.

Grandpa's life experience and Marine training gave him the exact tools he needed to train me so I would have the best chance to succeed. He did, however, have his work cut out for him as I was out of control. One of the first things Grandpa did when I moved in with him was send me to anger management classes. As an adult, I can understand my anger—the key is to have it under control.

Anger rarely serves anyone. However, I was never taught coping skills and effective ways to express my emotions. This is such an important skill to have in life, as everyone is faced with anger, and it is important to have a tool to help you manage it effectively.

My biggest takeaway from this time, which continues to change my life even today was learning how to have discipline and reward myself and others with the simple things.

Man, I miss him. I loved being around him and learning what kind of man I would become. I figured I'd probably be like him. I was just getting settled in and adjusting to losing Mom when I lost him, too. If I'd had my way, he would still be here giving me advice on my business and hopefully, he'd be proud of where I am in my life today. Do you have any special memories with a person you were close to? Close your eyes, and think of a good memory—these people and memories are your good cards. We have all lost someone. We should have gratitude for the good memories with them.

Grandpa was a hustler and fixer, always working on some sort of project. We spent many hours in his garage. Those lessons and memories are priceless and always put a smile on my face. Most of my tears have dried up when I think of him, and now I just get a warm, good feeling. Grief is like that. Death isn't.

Death can come out of nowhere—even on a regular day—when nothing special is going on.

Life changed again when Grandpa died. Our whole extended family used to take frequent road trips to visit family. It was important to Grandpa to share with the people he cared about the most the memories he was trying so hard to retain. Then the road trips stopped—Nana had too much to do raising my brother, cousins (who I consider more like siblings), and me as essentially a single parent (since my aunt lived there on and off)—there was no time or money for anything like that. I'm thankful that we always had the video recorder going when Grandpa was alive—maybe that was part of him being a mechanical engineer, or maybe that was his legacy—whether he intended it to be or not. Whatever it was, it preserved priceless moments I can revisit whenever I feel like it. The people I love the most are alive again in my mind and heart for those few minutes of film. My cousins and I still, to this day, will watch them on occasion.

It is because of Grandpa that I have a cherished recording of my mother dressed up as Santa Claus. I didn't believe in Santa Claus at a young age, and Grandpa tried to trick me into thinking that Santa Claus was real. That might be the most innocent and pure video that I not only own but have watched. There are lots of other types of videos of me being unruly and swearing. So, I especially like that innocent video—I can see the kid who should have had more time to just be silly, have fun, and play.

My upbringing with Grandpa taught me to be respectful of others and use manners. He taught me things like not to wear hats at the table and to keep your elbows off the table. He modeled what a good man was by respecting and honoring America when he volunteered for Missing In Action (MIA) soldiers.

Grandpa was simply the best father figure he could be in my biological father's absence.

Grandpa also taught me that respect is earned, not demanded. Let me give you a little context. People were messy when I was growing up. Or maybe I should say that people didn't keep the house the way I wanted. There were papers stacked and other clutter on the dining room table.

It always seemed some kind of cleaning could be done. What do you expect with all those people in the house? I didn't know how to rationalize that then, but I do know. Between the ages of 8 and 10, you could find me constantly cleaning and polishing. It was not as helpful as it sounds. I was a terror in every sense of the word and would swipe my forearm across the table and announce, "I cleaned the table. Respect me!" My cousin, who also lived in the home due to family misfortune, called me the Tasmanian Devil. I think I did things like that because I was overstimulated and did not know how to act, so I would act out with negative behaviors.

Remember, this was 20 years ago, and computers were barely in use, so let's cut Grandpa and Nana a break. Digital storage has changed everything. But seeing all of their papers on the table bothered me. There I was, learning to be disciplined and taking care of the yard, but I had to see all this junk in the place we should be eating our meals. It didn't make sense to me. Why weren't they just picked up? If the papers were put away, we would know where they were at all times. We wouldn't lose important documents. While we may have struggled in this area, in other areas, our surroundings were picture-perfect. What did your childhood table look like?

Modeling myself after my grandfather and conducting myself the right way, even today, is why I could push myself later in life. It is where my strength comes from when I have nothing left.

If I hadn't lived with my grandparents after Mom died, my life might have been different. Although I would like to think I had enough drive and desire to not end up being lost to addiction or turning to a life of crime. Nana and Grandpa gave me the foundational tools I would use to create a life that far exceeded the expectations the world had of me. This is the life I always knew I could achieve. Grandpa helped to make my journey one I could be proud of.

This is what I mean in saying your cards do not matter. You can always draw a new hand. It is in your control to do so. Each card has a different meaning and purpose—like the card that symbolizes my time with Grandpa.

The other epiphany I had was realizing that families look different for everyone. The rest of your life can look different, too. This applied to opportunities. It wasn't just that my personal life could go to shit. It was that it might take pretty damn miraculous upswings in the opposite direction. Learning this fact and looking forward to better days put an end to feeling sorry for myself. Now, I thought big. I thought *anything can happen, which means the good AND the bad*. It was a huge discovery—and it gave me the courage to finally take a chance on myself.

Indescribable (Nana)

Now, let me share with you about my Nana. Anyone who truly knows me knows how special my Nana was to me. Words simply do no justice to describe this woman. She was the matriarch of our family. My Nana was my best friend and, as I mentioned earlier in this book, my saving grace. She was the definition of unconditional love. Nana never gave up on me . . . ever! She was my number one fan and biggest supporter growing up, even when I did not deserve it. She was someone I could always count on and took the best care of me. I could do no wrong in her eyes. My family would all say, "Marc-y, you are Nana's favorite," but let's be real—I was.

Nana and I had a special bond. She was more of a mother to me than my own mother. She was one of a kind, and I am so blessed to have had someone as great as her raise me and help shape who I am today.

Nana was a tough cookie. She would give you the shirt off her back, but she also was a very strong and resilient woman. The cards she was dealt throughout her life are unimaginable, yet she put her life on hold for me, my brother, and my cousins.

After the tragedy of losing her husband, Nana was lost, lonely, and who knows what else. By then, she had the job of raising four kids without working outside the home. Unbelievably, she had lost four of her eight children and her husband, and then she was faced with being responsible for four more. There are not that many people who can put aside their agony to selflessly care for others in such a fashion.

My Nana knocked it out of the park! At 63 years old, she stepped up to the batter's box and provided us with the best life she could with what she had. She was taking care of teenagers and their varying personalities, which must have been tiring at her age.

Now, that is the definition of strength, determination, patience, and discipline all wrapped into one. We weren't the easiest kids to take care of either.

I never heard one complaint from Nana. She loved us all so much and wanted to see each of us succeed. She lived the last 18 years, dedicating her entire life to us kids. Everything went on hold, and she loved us with the warmest heart. Nana had such a funny personality of her own. She made the absolute best out of a situation that would've knocked down a much bigger person. She was set in her ways, but none of us would have wanted it any other way. Nana was Nana.

One of my favorite memories is going to yard sales with Nana. I watched her, along with other shoppers, argue down prices, which inspired my negotiation and sales skills! Nana lived a long life—fighting until the end when she knew everyone was safe and secure with their own families. Only after the new generation was ready for blast off did she sadly leave us. She would have adored all of her great-grandchildren. I swear she is watching down on us all.

The most fulfilling part of my journey so far is that I could repay her for everything she had done for us. I like to think I broke the family's curse by doing this and was able to make my grandmother financially free for the last five years of her life. She didn't have to pay her mortgage or any other bills ever again. Whatever she needed, I could build or provide.

Before she got very sick, I bought a home next door from where I was living at the time. It was a small one-level I had completely remolded with hopes for my Nana to move into. I bought it, so I could provide care for her 24/7. Unfortunately, by the time it was ready for her to move into, she was in and out of the hospital. She wanted to remain in the house where she'd raised us kids. That did not stop me from taking care of her for the remaining time she was with us. She was my world, and I will forever be thankful she gave us kids another set of cards after the first ones were dealt.

Losing my Nana was the hardest loss I've ever faced. Despite experiencing many tragic and painful losses, Nana's was different because she had always been there for me through everything. Her decline was particularly painful, and I spent many days driving back and forth to the hospital in Boston to be by her side. It was the least I could do after all she had done and sacrificed for me. Watching her decline was incredibly difficult, but I am grateful I could be with her in her final moments. Losing her left me feeling lost, but I knew she would want me to keep living and make her proud. She was always proud of me, and we had the best conversations. She remains my motivation, and I think of her every day.

When I reflect on my Nana and the profound impact she has had on shaping who I am today, I am filled with admiration for her nurturing spirit, boundless generosity, and the countless sacrifices she made for our family. She was a person who consistently put others before herself, a quality that never went unnoticed in my eyes. Nana faced many hardships with unwavering strength and resilience, qualities that deeply influenced me.

Witnessing her perseverance taught me the importance of not succumbing to self-pity or dwelling on adversities. Her strength instilled in me the understanding that life demands persistence and that two wrongs never make a right. This lesson has enabled me to let go of grievances and embrace kindness. Nana's example of selflessness and her belief in giving without expecting anything in return has profoundly shaped my approach to life. Her legacy of compassion and fortitude continues to inspire me every day, reminding me to be generous and kind regardless of the challenges I face. I will forever strive to make my Nana proud.

As we wrap up this chapter and move on to providing you with the tools you need to leave your legacy as Nana left me, let's talk about adversity and the takeaways you've learned that can become your tools.

Living with Adversity

You read about my adversity—a roller coaster of emotions for an adult, much less a child.

I needed to take time to sit with everything that had happened to me and get to a level of acceptance where I knew it would not get in the way of my goals.

If you are grappling with your adversities, I challenge you to speak to a professional, friend, or mentor so you will have a strong foundation to build the rest of your life on. It's time to put yourself first. Take the weight off of your shoulders as you give yourself room to live to your full potential.

Your past doesn't define you; you've been dealt a new hand NOW! Leave the old one where you found it.

If you are struggling to do this, let me remind you that you are alive and healthy. You are able to speak, think, move, and give back.

Remember this whenever you get stuck: Learn to let it all go.

If you're thinking *I can't* because life feels too heavy or overwhelming, let me assure you that "YOU can." Ask yourself: *what do I enjoy, and who do I want to be?* It is scientifically proven that you can retrain your brain and consistently overpower your negative thoughts. This is called neuroplasticity. Remember, you are not alone.

How many cards do you have in your hand? How many are in your deck? Just as we can't control what the dealer gives us, we cannot control what life throws at us. We tend to try and control certain situations because we can't control others. For example . . . I can control cleanliness. Therefore, I make sure my surroundings are clean. I couldn't control my childhood, but I could make sure that the dining room table was clean.

Building a New Routine

I challenge you to find a mastermind group like Apex, Uncaged, Arete, or even Facebook groups that you think you will enjoy. Start engaging with them. This will turn your mindset and social media feed into more positive posts, which will continue to motivate you.

It will also separate you from where you are now to where you want to go. Doing so might involve disengaging from friends and/or family if they have a negative impact on you. That's okay; it's time to surround yourself with positivity and winners. This is who you will transform into.

Next, I suggest following five influencers you can relate to, e.g., Andy Frisella, Ryan Stewman, Patrick Bet-David, Gary Vee, and so on.

Plan various tasks or activities that will push you forward daily. This might include going to the gym, getting reading time in, or even setting aside time to remember to be grateful. Get in the habit of self-care, and learn to be grateful for it.

These are just a few areas and goals of my life that can benefit you. Try to identify your own so that you can build a routine that you will take pride in following.

Think of one thing you want to implement and one thing you are grateful for. Sit down with someone in your life to talk about your childhood. Identify and sort through unprocessed and suppressed memories or events. Figure out the "why." Why do you tick the way you do? Why are you motivated in certain ways but not others?

As I've given you above, every chapter of this book will include tools that you can use to help you move forward.

See you on the next page!

2

It Was All a Dream

"Formal education will make you a living; self-education will make you a fortune."

—*Jim Rohn*

IF I WERE TO ASK YOU, "What is an entrepreneur?" what would be your answer?

Wix.com provides this well-thought-out definition: "Entrepreneurship is the process of creating, developing, and managing a new business venture with the aim of generating profits or creating value. An entrepreneur is an individual who takes on financial risks to start and grow a business, using innovative ideas and strategies to capitalize on market opportunities."[1]

Now, can you tell me what a dream is?

A dream to me is a personal vision of success. It inspires you to make more of yourself and achieve goals.

Do you remember the first dream you had? Do you still want to eventually reach it? Maybe your dream has changed? Your dreams and vision will develop alongside you.

Take a moment and think about said dream—whether it's an old or new one.

Some people have dreams of being an entrepreneur, and others need to use entrepreneurship as a vehicle to reach their dreams. The beautiful fact about life is that you can always change no matter your age.

How old people are when they go into business for themselves depends on individual experiences, influences, circumstances, and, of course, dreams.

In fact, as I sit here and write this book, I am sure that you can't have entrepreneurship without dreams. It is a requirement to know where you're going and why.

The most optimal way to operate your entrepreneurship is to blend your dreams with your mission. If you don't know how to do that, that's okay; keep reading, and I will give you more insight throughout these pages.

First, let me applaud you for working on your mindset at this point by picking up this book. You are the person I was

---

1   Cecilia Lazzaro Blasbalg, "What Is Entrepreneurship? A Complete Definition," Wix Blog, December 24, 2023, https://www.wix.com/blog/entrepreneurship.

thinking about when I decided to write this book. I know it's challenging to keep your dreams alive when all you can see are decades of an unknown future ahead of you. This chapter is designed to help you look past where you are currently through the insights I learned when working to rise above my circumstances.

I don't think we look at our past enough to see how it affects our future.

A Young Entrepreneur

My entrepreneurship seed was planted in middle school. I was selling DVDs, CDs, and ringtones to save money that I would then lend out to my family with interest! This is when I learned the power of money and that the more you have, the more you can create. Sounds crazy, right? But this is when it just clicked for me.

I have since found it easier to create more money than save it. I'll share more about this a little later. So, if you are curious about generating a stream of income that can alleviate many worries, keep reading!

After I graduated middle school, I started at vocational high school and continued my journey of hustling, working as a plumber, making very grown-up wages. In essence, I had two jobs: 1) a real job as a plumber and 2) my academic job as a student.

My dreams and success were all in my hands as soon as I was given the tools—which fueled my momentum. The taste of not having to fight so hard to save and scrimp was going away. I could see that, and I was not going to miss this one shot in my life to get ahead and get out from under. If I played my new cards right, I would never again have to go through the struggles I did when I was a kid.

I learned something else, too. Money made me happy, but I wasn't fulfilled. Fulfillment would come later. Fulfillment is connected to your purpose ("why") and your passion. It requires you to make plans and strategize so your earnings and opportunities will last a long time. You can learn about these concepts at any age, so don't hold back from getting started even if you think you are jumping the gun.

If you are reading this and building your road to entrepreneurship, remember that whether you are selling a service or a product in your new venture, the first sale is the hardest. Every sale after that will be easier—all because you have proved to yourself that you can do it. We believe we can't do things sometimes because we think other people are doubting us.

When your dreams seem to be out of reach, use any doubts as fuel for your first sale. Do you believe you can close that deal? If you don't, you won't. Don't sabotage yourself before you can even get started. Remove other people's opinions from your mind, as they do not matter. The only thing that does is what you believe you are capable of.

An old saying by Regina Brett, an American writer and inspirational speaker, goes, "What other people think of you is none of your business." Follow this advice as you build your dreams, and don't waste time on the opinions of others. Treat your opportunities as work in order to make money. Learn what you can from opportunity and how to handle financial gain. You will likely never go back to the way things were.

Let's be honest, you need money coming in the door to have a successful business. It has to be part of your dream. Don't skip thinking through this step. Come up with a foolproof way to nail it.

When I assess opportunity now, it is through multiple lenses (it is not through the opinions of others).

I decide if I should take it based on more than profit. Besides measuring a financial return, ROI (return on investment) can also mean getting back more respect and credibility through your actions, and it can give you opportunities to sit in rooms with other people. And you do want to put yourself in those rooms, no matter the size of your company. It is never too early to start branching out and meeting the influencers in your industry. Doing this can greatly influence how fast you grow.

I try to balance shiny object syndrome (being attracted to multiple things pulling you away from your main aim) and make sure that I won't deviate from pursuing my strategic goals.

The timing also has to be right. Most people overthink opportunities and don't act with speed. You're reading this book and are more likely to succeed than fail by that very act alone. Figure out if the timing is right, and if it is, act!

I ask myself, *is this going to make me happy?*

I read somewhere that when everyone is running in the same direction, to zig instead of zag. So, I think about if I will be able to do this, and if my research shows I likely can, then I know what I need to do: zig!

I assess what the opportunity will do for me. When you are weighing what to do next, make sure the terms will work for you. I am now conditioned to think, *what else is there to look at?* I make assessments based on experience and resources. I also fall back on my network—the people in my masterminds, for instance.

> *When I took out a loan for a restaurant, I knew it would lead to many more open doors, and how the loan was structured made it very hard to lose. I had never owned a restaurant.*

Hell, I had never even made mashed potatoes, but I had to find out if I would like owning one. I've since sold it at a profit. The point I want to stress is that we all need to find out what we do and don't like to make our direction clearer. Even if I had failed, I view failure differently now. Sometimes, you have to go through failure to get to success. You have to learn what opportunities will make you happy and feed you, and you can't do that without taking a chance. It's hard for entrepreneurs to say no, so go ahead and say yes to trying new things, but as you do, find what you like. Remember that your mentors are there to bounce ideas off of, too.

> *I seek mentorship when I am faced with making a decision (and even when I'm not).*

Doing so has served me well. When you are trying to decide whether to leap or hold back, practice setting aside your ego and normalizing getting help from mentors. If you are considering taking on an investment opportunity, as I was, make sure that you talk to other people. That first deal can seem daunting, just like that first client that you have to sell is—I get it. Part of that feeling comes from not having a frame of reference for what to do or if your actions or decisions are wise—until you talk to someone who's been there before.

Once I find a mentor, I do the research to feel good about working with them. The worst thing you can do is find somebody who you don't feel a synchronicity with. We all know those people who, when we talk to them, feel like our interactions are a skipping record. You want to work with somebody whose values you align with. That's just the start. They should feel approachable. They should have accomplished things in their life that you support and that you want in your life. They should be willing to hang in there with you when things get tough, and you're having a hard time choosing options A, B, or C. Your mentor should be well-versed in coaching you on how to move through challenges.

Motivation to Start Your Journey

As you read this book and think about your own dreams of starting your business and reaching your dreams, I want you to feel energized, motivated, and ready to challenge yourself to make a meaningful impact on your community.

This transformation will not happen overnight. Your foundation needs to be solid to gain momentum if you want to achieve your dreams. Remember, entrepreneurship can be a challenging path. It often gets harder before it gets easier. I promise you; I've walked in your shoes. You have a greater chance of lasting in business if you build a strong foundation.

Dreaming

Dreams have no restrictions—only the ones you put on them. Think back to the first significant dream you had. No matter if your dream has changed over time, the key is to understand what drives you.

My dream was to build a dominant organization surpassing anyone else's in my market and create a top workplace driven by company culture and personal growth. I wanted to impact many, not just a few.

After working for a large company for over a decade, I decided to pursue my dream of building my own business. In a conversation with a friend—now my business partner—we discovered that we both wanted to create a lasting legacy and shared the same core values. Realizing our shared vision, we decided to join forces and build a company where people would be excited to work and grow.

We committed to this ambitious goal and set out to create our dream, knowing it would require immense dedication and effort. Building our company demanded constant work and meticulous attention to detail to ensure smooth operations. However, the partnership thrived because we balanced each other well and we shared the same morals and values but brought different strengths to the table, allowing us to support each other and fill in the gaps as needed.

Our collaboration has been the foundation of our success. Together, we continue to build a company driven by our shared vision and commitment to excellence.

I want to help you structure your dream effectively so that it can become a reality. Some dreams are manageable, but others require a team. Waiting until you're knee-deep in running your business and working around the clock to make it profitable can lead to unnecessary challenges. Planning ahead can save you time, energy, and money. Running a business involves significant effort and many behind-the-scenes tasks to ensure smooth operations. Reliable and skilled team members are crucial for handling responsibilities effectively and on time. To grow, it's essential to have the right systems in place. My company's success is largely due to the outstanding team I have supporting it.

Dreams Don't Control You. You Control Them.

One of the most influential lessons I ever learned was that some people around me, while not intentionally trying to hold me back, even if they didn't make fun of my dreams, didn't seem to understand them. At the very least, they couldn't accept them. Their lack of belief in my dreams had everything to do with their lack of belief in themselves.

There is truth to the saying by our friend Jim Rohn: "You are the sum of the five people you hang around with."

So, distance yourself from people who might not serve you. Your dreams will never see the light of day unless you do.

I understand that when you start to mature, leaving behind some of the people in your friend group is hard. It might even feel like you're breaking your heart. But who you surround yourself with has everything to do with your journey and odds of success.

Ask yourself, *do I want to make a safe decision that will keep people in my life happy while it eliminates my chance of dreaming? Or do I want to use 10 seconds of bravery, sever ties with people who don't want to see me succeed, and give myself every chance of getting to the top?*

You will read about this point throughout the book. That is because you can't go any further down the path you want until you figure out who's supposed to be in your circle. What decisions are you making in this area that will impact your life negatively or positively? Take a moment to think about how what you decide will play out. Is it the right choice for you?

After my grandpa was taken out of this world, I can't begin to explain my level of anger. Not only did I lose him just like *that*, but I saw the whole thing. Too many people had dropped out of my life or disappointed me. I had been left yet again. I basically said, "Screw it," and I started getting in trouble with the wrong crowd. I was thankful that I was given the opportunity to go to Bristol Plymouth Vocational High School despite my poor grades and behavior.

Before my grandpa died, he told me, "This is where I want you to go. Your brother and cousin are already there, and I want you to follow in their footsteps." When I heard that, I knew I had to straighten up my act and start making better choices. I wanted to make Grandpa and Nana proud and prove that I was worthy of going there.

Back then, going to a vocational high school wasn't as popular as it is now. I was about to change out everyone surrounding me in favor of going to a new school, and many people couldn't understand why I was deciding to go there in the first place. Regardless of how others felt about it, I had to stay with my decision. I could feel that it was a step in the right direction.

The only thing that mattered was following the path to my dreams. I worked to develop a deeper relationship with my teachers, and they helped me get into Bristol Plymouth, which ultimately gave me the tools to ascend to a different level in life.

As you consider making these massive changes in your life, remember that only you can do the work that will move you forward. Your friends and family do not have the tools and means to make your aspirations happen.

Growing up, we may think, *if I make a mistake, I'll have plenty of time to fix it later.* I'm here to tell you that life is like dominoes. One decision connects to the next and the next. So, what if you played a different domino earlier in the game? What if you put yourself around the right people who believed in you and wanted to help you achieve higher goals? Wouldn't you get there quicker? Probably.

Maybe as you're reading this, you're thinking, *but I don't know what bad traits in other people I should watch out for.*

I got you.

Here are some characteristics in people that will drag you down—and this list is applicable to your group of friends, no matter your age:

1. Drug users.
2. Law-breakers.
3. Excessive partiers.
4. Nay-sayers.
5. Jealous individuals. Pro tip: Notice who is cheering around you and who isn't. Notice who is engaging with your posts about life going wrong and who is when life is going right.
6. Be mindful of energies such as those coming from a limited mentality or unmotivated people. Both are players in a dangerous game of cards. Shuffle them when needed and get a new hand.

Understand, though, that even if you know people with the above traits, it doesn't mean your friends are bad people. It means that if you want more out of your life, you have to get your need for immediate self-gratification and adrenaline-rushing under control—make sure the people around you are good for you—as you need to be for them.

People make all kinds of questionable decisions at all ages—myself included. That's called being human. If you read those questions and they rang a bell that something's not quite right, stop and improve your life.

Speaking of instant gratification, I had to get it under control if I ever wanted to make something of my life. In hindsight, I could see that retraining myself to move away from wanting what I wanted right then would take time. I was so anxious to get to a different place in my life. But I had to pace myself and be strategic, or what I was building wouldn't last or take me anywhere.

When you are resisting instant gratification, level with yourself and talk to somebody who can help you understand why you have such strong feelings. I also like to figure out why I want what I want when I want it.

What am I going to lose if I wait?

What part of me is fighting with myself, and why?

I have discovered that instant gratification doesn't usually have much to do with the thing you want.

You know how you feel when you get something new, and then after a few months, you don't care that much about it anymore? The key is to get to that stage *before* you buy the thing or derail yourself from reaching a bigger goal.

Controlling this gratification has to do with a feeling of lack or thinking you don't have enough, and sometimes, we bring that emotion forward from our childhood. Maybe we feel like we should have nice things now because we didn't then.

That's just one area you might need to work on. When you come from a rough childhood or a past riddled with pain, there are all sorts of ways you can doubt yourself. There are many other ways you can try to justify rash behavior. Get whatever you're dealing with under control because you can't build anything on a cracked foundation.

If you're embarrassed about your history, work on your self-talk, and don't keep secrets about your childhood. If you had a tough childhood, believe me when I say you had no frame of reference for higher learning or higher thinking. So, cut yourself a break already.

If you're in a depression, there are hotlines to call, or you can reach out to someone. Stay as busy and productive as much as you can.

Whatever you have to do, break through to the next level. There's nothing wrong with carving your own path— even if you have to leave a few people behind who weren't supporting you. It's totally worth it, I promise.

Besides leaving other people behind who don't support you, you also need to get rid of your negative self-talk. In this journey, you will change, and part of that change involves breaking away to find more supportive people and a healthier frame of mind. Fill your table with a circle that supports big dreams. Focus on topics like reading, mentorship, self-clarity, and working out.

When you take care of yourself, foundational items give you more clarity and a natural dopamine hit. Doing hard things not only creates more discipline but also opportunity. When you are your best self, you are able to impact others to do the same—you are creating positive effects.

Passion as the Driving Force

Ensure that you are genuinely passionate about whatever business or career path you choose—if what you are doing is tied to your dreams, this is likely the case. Try to avoid launching a business out of need or because you see someone else do it, but it doesn't set you on fire. Passion is your driving force. It will keep you motivated on days you're tempted to quit. A dream with baked-in passion can't be denied.

Don't be one of the people who make up this sad fact:

Most people don't enjoy their jobs. VeryWellMind reported in 2023 that "Nearly half of employees worldwide feel stressed at work while 40% feel worried, and 23% feel angry."[2]

When you become an entrepreneur, you give yourself an edge over half the world! That's a reason in itself to launch your dreams.

If you're confused about which passion to chase, I wouldn't worry too much. Many times, your passions will chase you! If you still can't nail down one direction, that might be an advantage, too. Some of the most profitable entrepreneurs have multiple pipelines of revenue coming in. That's a fact I don't have to provide a source for. I see it in my circles every day, and that's thinking big. If you can kickstart multiple pipelines, why wouldn't you take the chance to do so?

---

2   Rachael Green, "'I Hate My Job': How to Cope When You Feel This Way," Verywell Mind, May 16, 2023, https://www.verywellmind.com/i-hate-my-job-7485131.

The Power of Thinking Big

Most people are conditioned to be small-minded and play it safe. Small thinking guarantees stagnation. Understand that your "why" and purpose are interconnected. Knowing why you're doing something beyond just your end goal is crucial. For instance, you would not just run a business to pay your bills and make a living. Your purpose or "why" is usually bigger than yourself. It might have to do with taking care of your children or spouse. It might have to do with serving a larger cause than yourself.

Intertwine your "why" and passion as much as possible. Your passion will define your mission. When you identify it, it serves as a blueprint for your journey. That's the power of thinking big.

Imprinting a Legacy

It's never too early to think about the legacy you want to leave behind. Maybe your dreams hold a vision of a legacy you can't stop thinking about.

Your actions today will ripple into tomorrow and for years to come. I want to give my family and kids the keys to take their lives further than I did. I want them to challenge, impact, and build more opportunities for our community. How would you feel if you left an impact and legacy like Michael Jordan, Kobe Bryant, or Tom Brady?

When you begin working for yourself, you have all the ingredients to build a dream, legacy, and impact. Everyone out there who has achieved these goals started where you are right now.

Conversely, let's say you've lived a good chunk of life. If you're reading this book and feel like you're halfway through your days, remember that you still have the second half and can build it to be how you want it.

Let me give you an example. My good friend Eric, whom I look up to and who has taught me a lot over the years, will reach out to me for advice on occasion. When I was first getting into real estate, he was one of my go-to people for advice and questions. We flipped many houses together. A few years ago, he switched professions and went into the pipe insulation business. It's ironic because now the tables have turned, and I subcontract his business to complete repairs on my properties.

Eric recently called me and said, "Marc, we do business in totally different ways." He runs a smaller shop and wanted advice on what he felt I was dealing with in my team. "How do you hold your guys accountable in the field?" he said. I replied, "You have to build your business up around them, then go even higher. If you need to, get rid of the people who aren't working out and matching your core values and mission. That way, you can sustain."

What does your sustained future look like? A lot of what you do personally can affect you professionally. Remember, you are imprinting a legacy. What is your "why" to think ahead?

Eric talked about resisting technology, which I always try to embrace even though it might not be the most comfortable feeling. Still, it is necessary in this day and age if you want to build a lasting business. When I told him this, he said, "My kids won't want my business." To which I replied, "Stop thinking about yourself and your company as you run it today—as your vision. Your son might be on a mission to take it over and bring it to the next level with his vision. Get it ready for him."

I wish someone had told me 10 years ago to build my business so it's transferable to someone else. Implement the technology you can so when you hand it off, it'll be as easy as possible for the next owner—especially if they are a family member. Make it easy for others to pick up where you left off in your legacy.

What I've laid out here in this chapter will allow you to build your dream or dreams (if you're as crazy as me!). When you feel like too much information is coming at you, and you don't know which way to turn, come back here and re-read this chapter. Take it one section at a time until you feel comfortable.

Now, let's dive deeper into learning if you are excited about your dreams and want to jump right in without much planning or if your dreams crystalize through you mapping out lots of steps. Hint: Neither one is a right or wrong way to approach making your dreams come true, but knowing how you think and what you need is an undeniable edge.

Visionary and Integrator

Imagine your entrepreneurial venture as a machine with many moving parts. The Visionary is the dreamer who sees the big picture, future, and possibilities. They're the innovator, the idea generator, and the creative force behind your business.

The Integrator, on the other hand, is the operator who takes the Visionary's dreams and turns them into reality. They're the planner, the implementer, and the organizer, keeping the business running smoothly.

Which do you think you are? You might be surprised to learn the truth. So, let's go for it!

It's time to take the Visionary and Integrator Test.

This test is a tool that helps identify whether you lean more toward being the Visionary or Integrator. It's not about labeling yourself; it's about understanding your natural tendencies.

Some of us are born Visionaries, while others are born Integrators. Every successful venture needs both.

Recognizing these roles and their value allows you to focus on your unique strengths. I strongly encourage you to take the Visionary and Integrator Test. It's a pivotal step in preparing yourself for the path ahead. Understanding which of these roles fits you and, equally important, the roles you need to fill in your business will set you up for success.

What tools bring you enjoyment? I personally enjoy marketing. This will be the last position I will get rid of. Get your hands dirty, and delegate when needed. Everyone has strengths. Know them, work with them, and allow others to teach you something.

Head here to take the Visionary and Integrator Test:

https://rocketfueluniversity.com/quiz/
crystallizer-quiz-hs-norandom-privateapp.php

3

Unleash Your Entrepreneurial Superpowers

"Listen to yourself. Know what you want to be, and always be true about what you do."

–Unknown

HOPEFULLY, YOU TOOK THE TIME TO TAKE THE VISIONARY AND INTEGRATOR TEST at the end of the last chapter. If so, you now know more about how your mind works and your aptitude.

If not, please make time to take the test before you get too far along in the book. It is priceless to know how you operate and how you and others on your team can best serve your business.

Remember, there's no shame in needing help in certain areas, such as if you are mostly an Integrator and need help with the Visionary piece or vice versa. There is also no shame in not wanting to do specific tasks. I think of knowing what you want to do and the best place to put your efforts as power positions.

Please take a moment to consider the following:

- If you are a Visionary, your road and roles might include:

  ○ Thinking about where the business will be in 2, 5, or 10 years.

- If you are an Integrator, your road and roles might include:

  ○ Implementing a new payment processing system.

With the knowledge of who you are fresh in your mind from the results of your test, consider the additional strengths you will want to access as an entrepreneur. It takes the following traits to really pull it off.

Needed Entrepreneurial Traits

While I believe anyone can be an entrepreneur if they are hungry enough, these key traits will transition you from being good to great in your business.

#1: *Resourcefulness*

Resourceful people solve their own problems. They don't wait for direction from others, and so they collapse time, aka they get to their destinations and make discoveries sooner. If they want the answer, they will find it.

Being resourceful is the art of making the most of what you have, finding solutions when faced with challenges, and turning limitations into opportunities. In business, it's the difference between stumbling or leaping over obstacles. In life, being resourceful is your key to resilience and making the impossible possible. This isn't just a skill; it's a mindset. Master this, and you will transform any setbacks and detours.

In my mind, making mindset changes is an opportunity!

I once called out of work to take a 2-day real estate course. The people putting it on wanted me to spend $30k, but I refused. Instead, I attended the course, took what I learned, and put it to work for me. I had the mindset going into it to be as resourceful as possible.

Fortunately, we are living during a time when you have every resource at your fingertips to learn whatever you need to get ahead. All the top-performing athletes and celebrities have published their playbooks listing everything they did to get to the top. Use their knowledge to get ahead. Take the time to train yourself on anything you want to learn. I was once confronted with a 40-page report that I needed to provide feedback on. I remember receiving this report and thinking, *how in the hell will I complete this?* But I did it—one page at a time. Anytime you get overwhelmed, walk back a step, and chop up your tasks into more manageable pieces.

#2: Communication Skills

Communication is a superpower in business and life. It involves expressing yourself clearly, connecting with others, and turning ideas into actions. There's more to it than mere words; it's about making things happen. In business, communication is the secret sauce that helps you share your vision so you can lead your team. In life, it's your key to building strong relationships and turning dreams into reality. When great communication is topped with sales experience, it is the recipe for winning.

#3: Organization

Organization is the skill of arranging things neatly, staying on top of tasks, and turning chaos into a plan. It isn't task management; it's creating a clear path to success. In business, it's your blueprint for efficiency and growth. In life, it's your secret to managing time, reducing stress, and achieving your goals. Most business owners have trouble with their work-life balance. Learn to be organized, as it will reduce your chances of falling short in this category, making you and everyone else in your circle happier.

#4: Coachability

Being coachable is your ticket to furthering growth in business and life. It's the ability to listen, learn, and adapt with an open heart and mind. Coachability means you are committed to becoming a lifelong learner. In business, being coachable is the key to unlocking your full potential to collaborate with mentors and adapt to any changes in plans. In life, it's your path to personal growth. It takes continuous improvement to build the life you want. That's not to say you can't fall off the path once in a while. If you do, just get back on. You can't create anything of worth if you're a know-it-all who refuses to absorb helpful information that can put you on the map.

That might be easier said than done. We can tend to allow our ego to get in the way of making the correct decisions. It's natural to defend your positions and opinions. It's a very primal urge taken to protect yourself. But you can recondition yourself to react differently and receive information openly.

At all times, strive to do what is best for the team or your goals. One of my business's core values is putting the team's needs before personal needs. I need to remain coachable and maintain perspective in this area if I am going to operate a healthy business. I encourage you to make your decisions in the same way.

#5: Vision

We've talked about having a vision, so I will keep it brief here. Here are the high points: You can't open a business without knowing what you want, and you need to do something you love if you expect your business to last. As you contemplate operating a business, ask yourself what you are passionate about. If you don't do something you love, you won't be as successful—you are also more likely to experience burnout. Tap into your passion early and often. I recently exited a business because I didn't love it. If you don't have a passion for your business, it isn't *if* it will end; it's *when*.

Vision is the destination; it's up to you to create the direction. Vision is the ability to dream big, so set your eyes on the trophy, and turn your imagination into reality. In your everyday life, vision is the reason you wake up with excitement and purpose. It is your driving force.

#7: Self-Discipline

Discipline is the power to remain focused, using good habits to conquer your goals. There is a difference between discipline and motivation. Discipline is not punishment—it is doing what you need to do at the moment to gain a greater goal. It is built on long-term actions. Motivation is a burst of energy and inspiration. It involves taking short-term actions that don't necessarily renew themselves or contribute to the future.

As you move along on your entrepreneurial journey, you'll need to continually find the motivation to keep going while holding yourself accountable to do what you said you would do. Motivation and staying focused go hand in hand. I can stay focused because I am competitive, which allows me to laser in on my goals. I also know that people count on me for their everyday needs, so my obligations are to win and be the best I can be, not just for me but for them. When you find your passion, focusing on it is effortless. It truly doesn't feel like work.

Speaking of staying on track, ask yourself the following, and be honest about the answers: Where have you been unmotivated and lacked discipline? Strategize to overcome your obstacles through discipline.

Putting yourself under a microscope can be scary. Don't be afraid to learn about what you can do to get better. You have to make sacrifices to achieve what you want. You'll have to give up some social or family events, for instance, in favor of work. That's discipline, and it's a part of being a business owner. Remember what you are trying to build—and be okay with the occasional compromise to get there.

#8: Resilience

Resilience is a key to success. It allows you to grow through adversity and overcome hardships—exactly what you are setting out to do in this book.

Going after your dreams and starting and running a business will be stressful at times, and you have to learn how to reinforce your strengths to power through it. Not everyone is built this way, and some people will have to work harder to develop this trait. That's okay.

Being a successful business owner requires consistency, mostly entailing working 16-hour days in and out of the office to accomplish all the tasks that need to be done. At times, I am answering emails or preparing for meetings or other projects from home. After many years of this schedule, I have learned that how you think about additional work has everything to do with how you frame it. This is why I advocate practicing gratitude—you will understand the difference between *having* to do something and *getting* to do it. I get to build my business. I get to have this life.

Everything you need to build up or work to uncover within yourself is okay. Even if you discover as you are walking the path of entrepreneurship that it's not for you, that's alright, too. Be resilient enough to bounce back from the steps you took to get started. If you find this is your right path, stay the course. It's not easy, but this is part of being a resilient entrepreneur.

Be open to exploring who you are, and always be true to yourself.

The ability to bounce back from setbacks, adapt to change, and grow stronger is your weapon for navigating daily business challenges.

You can build resilience by being around people who care about you and removing those who don't. Resilience has to do with your mental and physical health, too. Take care of yourself by eating well, staying active, and getting enough sleep. It is easy to fall into bad habits; that is why it is so important to stay consistent and follow good habits. Whenever I go to the gym and eat well, I feel my best.

Reinforce your ability by achieving small, doable goals and celebrating them. Stay positive and consistently practice, getting better in every area you need to. You will win with consistency.

Good ideas are only good when you use consistency, so strive to be consistent in all areas of your life. When you do, areas where you might be struggling will improve. The other improvements will come with experience.

The Four Core

I've identified four core areas where you need to build resilience and have included examples of habits you can practice and questions you can answer. The four core areas are: Family, Fitness, Finances, and Faith.

1. Anticipate there will be problems across each of these four areas, so strive to always be prepared versus reacting to events. For example, what would you do if you couldn't get the funding you anticipated to pay a new vendor? If you screwed up the time for a very important call you scheduled with a major prospective

client? If someone on your team dropped the ball on a pivotal project? Thinking of how you will react isn't gloom and doom. It keeps you on point to better handle eventualities. Hey, you're running a business. Shit is going to hit the fan every now and then!

2. Be ready when it does.

3. We are all changing at every moment of every day in each of these areas, and these changes add up over time until, eventually, who you were several years ago is vastly different from who you are now. Who you are today before you start your business and let the world know this is what you want to do is not the same person you will be when you open your doors—or years down the road after you have some real experience under your belt. Pay attention to these changes and use your tools to make the best decisions possible.

4. Prepare for what will happen once you tell people about your business plans. Some will look at you differently. They won't see the you they are used to seeing. They may object to the dreams you share with them. Try not to take it personally, and remember, they haven't learned what you know and will look at you through that lens of not realizing what you are doing is possible, or they might think it doesn't make sense. When I was writing this book, I had to put myself out there and let people know this was what I was doing, subject to some opinions. I had to ignore any jealousy or resentment they may have been feeling. Always practice your resilience, and keep your faith.

5. When changing who you are and what you are doing, establish authority. Sometimes, your message will hit people it's not intended to, which might ruffle some feathers, but remember, this is none of your business. Navigate your road, and kill them with kindness,

remembering as you do just how resilient you are becoming. In the words of my wise cousin Shantel, "Kindness should be a way of life, not a strategy." If you are kind, you will relate to the correct audience. You will not have to search as hard to find the people you want to work with.

6. Establish a good support group with your family and friends. Doing this can create mind-blowing results.

7. Always try and pull people up with you. When you find like-minded people, make sure to give them a hand. Strive to create a symbiosis where you help each other. I always give people my secrets and don't worry about them knocking me down; as I know, only 1% will ever do anything with what you tell them.

#9: Speed

I have had major success operating with speed. Speed means acting and achieving your goals with efficiency. This isn't about rushing; it's about seizing opportunities and making the most of every second you have. Anyone who works with me knows that this is how I operate. Some may think that I go too fast, but this is what I have to do to get to that next level.

In business, speed is your competitive edge, allowing you to stay ahead of the curve and capitalize on opportunities before others catch up.

To maximize your time, use a calendar. It will allow you to operate with more speed and less procrastination, creating additional time with your family and friends. This is non-negotiable for me. I even tell my wife if she needs me to do something, to add it to the calendar. She knows the drill.

With all that I have going on in my life, it is easy to oversee and forget about something or overbook. If something is on my calendar, I know it will get done and not forgotten. I try and make life easier by using all these tools on a daily basis and like to stay consistent, as I said earlier.

If you're struggling with acting quickly, keep in mind that procrastination is a shadow of depression. It will silently steal your time. It's the habit of delaying action and will do nothing for you. Embrace the fact that the only thing that cannot be bought on earth is TIME, and commit to never wasting it as much as possible. Life is short; you need to make the most of it while you can!

I have found in my entrepreneurial ventures that the one who acts with speed usually wins. So, get started now. Find your playbook now. There's no reason to wait. Don't procrastinate because there will always be a reason why it feels like it's not the right time. Everyone always waits for the right time to buy a house, but the market increases yearly. And you can apply this analogy to so many things: buying a car, starting a family, getting an education, etc. There is never a perfect time; you will adapt and make it work.

You can plan to the best of your abilities, but there will always be variables. Learning how to act quickly instead of waiting for everything to be perfect is part of growth, and when you master it, it's a superpower. Allow yourself to fail fast and recover quickly. You can't succeed without putting in the work or taking the shot.

#10: Passion

We did a deep dive into this already, but it belongs on this list. We can't leave it out. If you are an entrepreneur, you need this burning fire, or you can't play the long game.

Passion keeps you coming back for more and more, even when you would rather take a break. The beauty of passion is that you can pause and then return to the work later—not only that, but you will *want* to return to it. Here's a spin on a Banksy quote: "Passion allows you to rest, not quit."

Do what you love, and it will never feel like work. When you find something you are passionate about, you will be all-in. Many people are money-driven, but you can make money in any industry as long as you are innovative enough. Look at Dollar Tree . . . How do you make money selling items for one dollar? But they are able to do so.

Mental and Physical Challenge

The 75 Hard Program is a popular self-improvement challenge created by Andy Frisella, a prominent entrepreneur and the CEO of 1st Phorm International. It is designed to foster mental toughness, discipline, and personal growth.

These are the key components of the 75 Hard program:

Daily Diet: Participants must follow a strict diet with no cheat meals, no alcohol, and no junk food for the entire 75 days. They should focus on clean eating, proper nutrition, and staying hydrated.

Two Workouts: Every day, individuals must complete two separate workouts. One of these workouts should be outdoors and last at least 45 minutes, regardless of weather conditions. The other workout can be indoors and should last at least 45 minutes.

Read 10 Pages: Participants are required to read a minimum of 10 pages from a non-fiction, self-help, or personal development book each day. The goal is to encourage daily learning and personal growth.

Drink One Gallon of Water: Staying properly hydrated is essential. Participants must consume one gallon (128 ounces) of water daily.

Take a Progress Photo: Every day, participants must take a progress photo to document their physical transformation throughout the challenge.

No Alcohol or Cheat Meals: As mentioned earlier, the program strictly prohibits alcohol consumption and cheat meals for the entire 75 days.

Stick to the Plan: If a participant fails to complete any of the daily tasks or violates any of the program rules, they must start over from Day 1. This challenge requires strict adherence.

Now that you have worked on your mental toughness, it's time to take a deeper dive into honing the vision for your business, which we will do in the next chapter. Keep going!

4

Ignite the Vision, and Defy Adversity!

"Vision without action is merely a dream. Action without vision just passes the time. Vision with action can change the world."

–Joel A. Barker

I TOUCHED BRIEFLY ON THE VISION REQUIRED TO BE AN ENTREPRENEUR, but vision is so important that it deserves its own chapter.

You must be able to see it in order to be it!

Vision is the hardest part of the entrepreneurship journey to define. That means it's even more important for you to take the time to deliberately identify your vision and what you want to do.

Sit down and work through what you want to do and where you want to go. Resist the urge to let yourself get scattered by tapping into different ideas that you know will take you away from your main purpose.

Because I have multiple businesses, I have multiple alter egos and visions. You might be in the same boat, and I can offer you guidance if this is the case. All you have to do is keep reading.

We will dive into implementing your vision shortly, but before we start, I want to clarify the two crucial roles of entrepreneurship once more—so the definitions and differences of the Visionary and Integrator are fresh in your mind.

The Differences

The Visionary is the creative dreamer who generates innovative ideas, sees the big picture, and sets the course for the business. They imagine the future and provide the inspiration.

The Integrator is the detail-oriented executor. They take the Visionary's ideas and turn them into reality. Integrators ensure that strategies are implemented, goals are met, and operations run smoothly.

An Integrator can also be quite useful if you're having a hard time clarifying your vision. As the more practical thinker, they can get you to think about your dreams less emotionally and help you to sharpen your vision so it is easier to understand, then the Visionary can implement it.

The difference between the two lies in their strengths and areas of focus.

Are you a Visionary or an Integrator?

Have you uncovered your vision? Let's unlock the true potential within you. If you haven't yet, you may want to head back to the end of Chapter 2 and click the link to take the Visionary and Integrator Test.

Now, let's talk about defining your vision.

What Do You Want, and What Are You Good At?

Do you envision a sprawling empire, or do you see yourself as the CEO of a venture with a handful of dedicated employees?

The first step in your entrepreneurial journey is finding your passion—the driving force that will propel you toward your destination. But passion is not enough; you need a map, a blueprint to turn your dreams into reality. This map is your vision, the cornerstone upon which every successful journey is built. You must operate with purpose, speed, and relentless determination—and you can only do that with a defined vision.

Even though I scored high as both a Visionary and Integrator, sometimes I don't know which angle to take and how to visualize my efforts. I am pulled in two different directions. Sometimes, it is a good problem to have, and others, I would like a little more clarity about the next step to take.

Figuring out my next move can take a lot of alone time. I like to embark on a day-long journey of solitude from everything and everyone to clear my head. If this appeals to you, and you need a breather to get clear, go for a walk in the park, go for a drive, or get a hotel room and sit in solitude without all the distractions. When you turn down the volume on the world, you can disconnect to face the reality of what you want and figure out how to get it.

As you are working to refine your vision, get honest with yourself. Not everyone is good at everything. That is the brutal truth, but once again, the sooner you can accept it, the sooner your life will change. You will stop beating your head against the wall in certain areas where you will just more naturally struggle. You might be more right-brained than left-brained, for example. That's completely normal, so don't spend time overthinking about it. Use your time wisely to take steps along your path.

I know it is so easy to get caught up in what other people are doing and think because they are all great at basketball; for instance, you should be, too. But you just might not be, and that's okay. You're probably great at a lot of other cool things. In fact, I know you are!

Go after what you are talented in. Look at yourself in the mirror and ask yourself, *is this what I really want?* And *how hard do I want to struggle in this area when this other area feels easier and less* forced?

When you work in what you're good at, you will find ways to make yourself enjoy it. You will have the motivation to educate yourself when needed; you will seek out resources without being asked, and you will have an innate curiosity that will propel you to greater heights.

I am deeply passionate about my work and am committed to continuous learning and growth. I actively participate in various groups and programs, where I am surrounded by like-minded individuals who share this dedication. Through these interactions, I have cultivated a global network of friends and colleagues who offer valuable advice and tools. It's invigorating to engage with people from diverse backgrounds, many of whom I don't see regularly. This fresh perspective is not only enriching but also essential for my personal and professional development.

Learn the difference between stress versus pressure as you progress. Adjust fire when and where needed. Simply: stress is bad, and pressure is good.

Once you condition yourself to work under pressure, you can execute to win much more often. It's easier to get better results when you are executing to your strengths.

More Help

If you need further help to drill into your vision, consider using a vision board. My friend and vision board coach, Steve Gamlin, offers this advice for successfully using a vision board:

The following is from Steve's Visualize in 5, a coaching tool outlining "5 Quick Steps to Build & Boost Your Visualization Muscle." Ask yourself:

Step 1: What do you want?

Wherever you are in life, chances are you'd like to *be* something else, *do* something else, or *have* something else.

It's all part of being human, and by no means is that a sign of weakness or failure. If you seek to upgrade your life in some way, it means you are still breathing, driving, and striving! So, what do you want to do, be, or have that will be an improvement over where your life is right now? If it seems overwhelming, pick just ONE thing in one area.

It could be money.

Your weight.

Your job.

The emotions you feel most often.

Your home.

Your car.

Your closest relationships.

Anything.

What does it look like, feel like, sound like, or even smell like . . . right now? And how would you like that ONE thing to be in the future . . . say, a year from now? Describe it in detail as vividly as possible. Today . . . and in the future. This will become the foundation for your first visualization.

Step 2: Why do you want it?

Please do us both a favor and do NOT answer: "Because a TV commercial made it look sexy!" Of course, it did. That is a commercial's job. I'm talking about a gut-level "why," one which affects you on a deeply emotional level.

Tune out all the "noise" around you and keep asking yourself, "why?" until you strike the "emotional" gold that will keep your fire burning and help you take consistent action. Your "why" will be the flame that keeps your path well-lit when self-doubt and confusion threaten to shut you down, when other people try to run you off your own rails, or when popular opinion dictates that you should quit. Eliminating the noise allows you to be more in control to clarify your future. What is noise to you in your life right now? Parents? Feeling stressed? Being bullied? Write down your noise.

Your "why" is just that . . . it's *yours*.

So, for the item you selected in Step 1 . . . what is your "why?"

Please note: You may have to ask yourself more than once. My personal record is asking myself 17 times "why" I made a certain choice in my life. And the answer is still keeping me going several decades later. So, what is your "why" for the answer to Step 1?

Step 3: Who already has it?

If you want it, chances are someone else already has achieved it. That statement probably covers 99.9% of goals, hopes, and dreams out there. So, who inspired YOU to want it? How did they achieve it? What did they read? Who inspired them? Who showed them the way? What resources did they engage?

The people who are where you wish to be have left clues. They have written books or blogs. They've recorded podcasts or been interviewed on radio shows. They've produced videos or tutorials.

Do you know how to find them? They may be internationally famous, or they may live in your hometown. The knowledge is yours for the asking. Are you willing to dig deep and put in the work to get there yourself?

Step 4: Who are you?

Now, be honest. Are YOU the type of person who will get out there and do what other people did to achieve the results you're after? Are the necessary mindset and behavior patterns part of your arsenal?

If not, you have two choices: Either change your behavior or surround yourself with the people who can help you get there.

This can be a tough question to answer for many people who refuse to dig deeply enough to see if their wiring is helping or hindering them. You can't procrastinate your way to success. You can't just wish for it, either. Someone has to do all the work, and you need to be part of the process, even if it just means being captain of the crew who helps you to get there. So, take charge, starting today, by answering: "Who are you?"

Step 5: What is your next *step?*

Think of your life as a treasure map. Your goals, hopes, and dreams are represented by a big red X in the sand, somewhere in the distance. You know where they are, and you know where you are right now. There is space in between. That space will be populated by the decisions you make and the actions you take. Not sure what to do first? Start at the X, saying to yourself: *If I achieved this, I must have done this* (identify an action step).

Then, keep taking one step backward at a time, asking that same question over and over again until you get where you are right now. Not sure what some of these steps might be? Go back to Step 3 and do some additional digging. Reach out to people. Study their words, their steps, and their stories. The knowledge you seek is out there. And please remember this most important part: *keep moving!*

Your Visualize in 5 Action Guide

Write out the above questions, and using one of your goals, proceed through the five steps. This is a sampling of the deep-diving knowledge delivered inside the *Vision Board Mastery* program and reinforced by the *Vision Board Mastery Group Coaching* program.

So . . . put pen to paper. Somewhere along the way, you will see and feel your path to that X (one of your most desired outcomes) getting more real and defined. Write in the margins. Flip the page over, and use the back if you need to. Go wild, and have fun!

If a conversation would help, go to SteveChats.com, *and let's discuss how you can go from where you are right now . . . to where the BEST VERSION OF YOU resides and thrives!*

Support Your Vision

Some people get all tangled up when they are weighing what to do. They look so many years ahead of themselves and can't imagine taking such a big leap to get there from where they are.

Dreams start in the present.

Plot out the paces to move forward to the extent that the dream you've held out in front of you seems possible. If you can't envision the path, that doesn't mean you can't walk it.

The goal is to fail fast and do 50 things wrong, so you can get them out of the way. You just want to hit on the one right thing to bring you to success. That's all you need. Focus on that little number. Know it's possible. After all, you can't succeed without putting in the work. Remember these three steps to creating your vision: 1) passion, 2) action, 3) execution!

Tips to Help You Achieve Your Vision

1. Your vision can be discovered through life adventures, daily activities, emotions, friendships, learning, schooling, what your parents are teaching you, etc. Your tools for creating your vision evolve as you grow and change over time. Everyone has a vision when they are a kid. You might have grown up wanting to be a cop, a firefighter, a doctor, a veterinarian—it doesn't matter. We all had visions that may not make sense now that we are older.

2. Surround yourself with the right people who will help you support your vision. This is not the time to hear anyone talk down to you about what you want to do. Ideas come to fruition through communication. The more people you listen to, the more you will see the steps you need to take to create it, and the more real it will be. Don't be afraid to brainstorm about your vision with people, too. Just refuse to be swayed to their vision, and stick to what you know you want in your heart. Brainstorming with the right people can truly help you get unstuck and learn what other people see in you that you might be a little blind to.

3. Trust yourself to bring your vision to life. Just like this is not the time to entertain the doubts of others, it is not the time to let your personal doubts run rampant, either. Doing that won't serve you at all.

4. Seek to create solutions. Always look at how to improve your vision or someone else's (if you are innovating it). As you are creating your vision, recognize that you will need help to clarify what you need to do next. Getting input from other people who have built what you are trying to or who have been on a similar path will shortcut your failures and keep you away from distractions that won't serve you. Ask questions and for the resources you need. Requesting these things will save you time and wrong turns more than if you were to do it on your own.

5. Back to those four fundamentals: Family, Fitness, Finances, and Faith to get mentally and physically ready to own and run a thriving business, operating at the highest levels of life.

   a. Family: Who are you hanging around? How are they influencing you? Are you a taker, or are you giving beyond your capabilities and emotionally exhausting yourself? Assert your independence and stop relying on your family if possible. Remember, the one who gives the most wins.

   b. Fitness (health and nutrition): Have a regimen for your fitness and nutrition. Don't eat garbage. Move your body. Lather, rinse, repeat. If you are not putting good fuel into your body or going to the gym regularly, eventually, you will struggle to keep up when you are trying to grow and scale.

   c. Finances: Get your financial house in order. Pay your bills, and make smart decisions. Resist spending for instant gratification. If you owe a ton of money on credit cards, you haven't achieved optimum performance in this area. Work on it and get better.

    d. Faith: What is your attitude and perception? It helps to give your worries and challenges to a Higher Power, and it keeps you humble.

6. If you don't have a vision, it doesn't eliminate you from being an entrepreneur; it might just take some work or meditation to dig it up. But you can also become an intrapreneur. An intrapreneur is a person who is able to develop a new project or venture within an established business while using the company's resources, so they don't have to fully launch on their own and endure the risks of full entrepreneurship. Channeling your passions into this line of work can save you the time of creating an entire company while still offering you freedom and ownership of your role.

New Possibilities

If you are dealing with a raging case of imposter syndrome, you should know that we have all been there. Second, I once heard that imposter syndrome means you care deeply about the quality of whatever you're working on and how people will be affected by what you share. It means you want to do a good job. That's a great sign of your integrity. So, instead of kicking yourself for feeling this way, pat yourself on the back!

Let me transport you back to my journey of finding my vision. My vocational high school years unveiled new possibilities in my life. Opportunities arrived, and I seized them with open arms. As I graduated high school with a diploma and the hours required for my plumbing license, the pieces began falling into place. My journey is a testament to the importance of following the action steps outlined in this book; opportunities will knock, but it's your responsibility to answer and seize them. I was determined to stay the course, and three years later, I achieved a milestone—I became the first master plumber to obtain a license at my trade school.

This accomplishment infused me with momentum. Soon, another opportunity materialized, and I entered the realm of real estate. You see, entrepreneurs are relentless—we always crave more! That's what was feeding me: whatever was next for me. If you are fighting these feelings inside, know that you can use them to your advantage and build, build, build! Create success!

Fast-forward a decade, and not only have my partners and I built a 75-employee HVAC organization from scratch, but I've also dived headfirst into real estate. I've since fixed and flipped over 250 properties, and plans for developing 60-plus units in the next 12 months are well underway. Our passive income portfolio boasts nearly 50 units—all from humble beginnings and a spark of vision.

I've reached financial freedom, and I'll say it louder so you can really hear it this time: YOU CAN, TOO!

Life sometimes presents you with an opportunity too good to let slip through your fingers. I was determined not to pass up these prospects, but my motivation went beyond an immediate gain—there's that training yourself to reject instant gratification that we talked about.

I saw these opportunities as steppingstones, each one leading to greater heights, and I embraced the challenge, jumped from the plane, and constructed the parachute on my way down—breaking the shackles of childhood adversity and waiting until the time was right to capitalize.

Never turn down an opportunity. This is an entrepreneurial hack. Opportunity leads to ideas where innovation can lead to success. Doors will open!

As you breathe life into your vision, your knowledge will expand, and your network will flourish, leading to a significant increase in your net worth. But there's a secret ingredient to supercharge your journey—FOCUS. What you focus on becomes reality.

When you create a vision board and speak about your goals daily, you breathe your dreams into reality. So, please make sure you go through the vision board exercise. You will be surprised at how effective it is—especially when you FOCUS. In other words, don't you dare take your eye off the prize.

5

The Heartbeat of Your Business: Core Values and Your Mission Statement

"The true test of a person's character is how they behave when no one is watching. Their core values are revealed in those moments."

—Roy T. Bennett

THE QUOTE AT THE TOP OF THE PAGE defines core values and applies to both the personal and business aspects of them—as seen through the eyes of one person. Still, it's one of the best definitions I have read.

I like this definition of personal core values from betterup. com: "Personal values are a set of beliefs that differentiate between 'good' and 'bad' in your community, culture, or society. They form a mindset that defines what you view as the ideal standards of behavior, like patience and honesty."[3]

In this chapter, we are continuing our journey into the heart of your entrepreneurial venture. We will explore the significance of your core values and mission statement. These foundational elements will not only serve as your guiding principles but also as the beating heart of your business; they will guide your every decision and action.

Do not skip the step of identifying and writing out your core values and mission statement. I can't stress this enough.

Understanding Core Values

It's crucial to familiarize yourself with the principles that make up your very core before you take the first step of opening your business. Your core values and mission statement will reflect what you believe in and how you will approach life's challenges. They will govern your personal and business life—yes, your friends and family can also be fired.

But Why Are Core Values Important?

Core Values help us make choices that align with our authentic self and long-term vision. When you stray from your core values, things don't often go how they should. It's

---

3   "What Are Personal Values? 20 Examples & Ways to Find Yours," BetterUp, accessed May 8, 2024, https://www.betterup.com/blog/personal-values-examples.

similar to being on a ship with no captain. As a leader, you need to create, lead, and live by these values to find success.

Personally, your core values should familiarize you with your inner workings. You can't not know how you tick. Some people don't take the time to understand their values and then wonder why certain events in their lives went wrong. I am giving you a heads-up, so you don't make those mistakes. Missteps are preventable if you know to avoid them.

A great way to start writing out your core values is to consider how people around you perceive you. Their feedback offers valuable insights into your actions and words. Take note of their observations, as this exercise can unveil areas where your actions align or conflict with your intended values. At the base, you want to answer: What do you stand for, and what are your non-negotiables?

Core values should align with your vision, personal attributes, and faith (if applicable). Of note, creating a solid and healthy company culture springs from identifying the right core values and their proper implementation.

Before we put pen to paper, let's go a little deeper into the impact of your core values.

How Core Values Relate to Culture

When I sat down to write this book, I had to figure out what culture means to me. I know what I want to see in the workplace and how I want employees to feel, but trying to define it and compartmentalize it was another story. It's not a black-and-white issue.

My unofficial definition of culture is that it is the base of my expectations for my clients, employees, and myself. Culture is the culmination of identifying a vision and incorporating it into your core values.

When I was 28, I started thinking about the culture I would cultivate in my future business. Most people don't think about generating a positive culture until they are in the thick of it, and then they have to be reactive to what's happening around them in their business. I didn't want to have to deal with that—or put anyone else through that unnecessary stress, either.

When people don't sit down and dedicate the time to developing their culture and core values, they aren't putting any thought into their or their employees' expectations, and that can spell trouble.

I was exposed to the wrong way businesses took care of themselves and their employees—or didn't. That's when I determined this would never be how I operated. I didn't want what not to do to become the norm in my world. I didn't want to fix issues that didn't need to exist if I'd just put the right people and building blocks in place.

Because culture is so hard to define, let me give you some points to consider. When you answer these questions, you will get a better idea of the type of culture you can create:

1. Do you want to have company events?
2. Do you know what your marketing will look like and what you want to be known for?
3. When you put your messaging out there, you tell people what kind of company you have. You are letting them know what it's like to work for you. When you do this right, and people see you, they will want to be you. So, what kind of messaging will you share?

4. Are you cultivating conditions suitable for growth, trust, communication, and loyalty for your employees? Are you demonstrating you are who you say you are?
5. What can you do to boost morale?

Be an organization that looks out for its employees. I have always wanted a company with our values. My goal was for people to walk in smiling and happy to go to work. If this doesn't happen, I'm not doing my job.

I know now that identifying your core values and mission statement leads to your culture. Blend in automation and speed, and you've got yourself a resilient company.

I'm not doing what other HVAC companies around me are doing. As I look around, I see that they're dying out. I don't want that to be my legacy. My tactic has always been sacrificing profit for happiness, but these other companies around me are doing it the opposite way. I figure how I'm proceeding is the new way of thinking. You can't get any simpler: Just follow your happiness and what you know will be the best for your team. That is the basis of our culture. It keeps people happy and performing. They take pride in their work, and happy employees equal a thriving company employing lifers.

Happiness and emotional and structural integrity go hand in hand, regardless of if you have 5 or 100 employees. Just know the moment you take on your first new hire—it will change you. So, get ready for that. Put yourself in a better position at every stage of your business, now and in the future. Know exactly what your plans are and what they will accomplish for your staff and company.

If you have a business mindset and think that not choosing profit will hurt you in the industry, understand there is more fulfillment in seeing your team win.

Culture applies to more than just you. It affects everyone and everything in your business. It calls for you to pay attention and operate consistently. As you are growing, multiple employees will increase your revenue, and you need to be able to fire on all cylinders at all times. Don't lose your grip on your culture when you start to grow. Stay credible by sticking to your core values across all areas of your business.

Learn to see and hear your employees. This is crucial as employees deserve to feel heard and seen. Know that everyone wants to be a part of the team. It is your job to nurture that. It is your job to understand that the most important person in your business is the one answering the phone. No matter what job a person holds, they deserve the utmost respect—whether they are the CEO or janitor. Titles are less important these days, anyway, so don't get weighed down by old ideas of hierarchy in business. Get in the trenches with your team and encourage them to communicate what's important. Learn your employees' love languages.

Part of leading employees is learning to deliver what means the most to them in the way they want to receive it. In other words, some people are more appreciation-driven while others are money-driven. Knowing what drives employees helps them feel understood, and it gives me the information I need to keep them happy. Work to develop this trait as an entrepreneur. You will need many skill sets. This is one of them.

To memorize my employees' love languages, I write up a player profile for each employee and commit to learning it.

This little rundown includes their name at the top of the page and questions like:

- What is his/her favorite place to eat?
- What are his/her kids' names?
- What are his/her dreams?
- What do they want in their role and in this business?

Take a moment and answer those questions, and you will have a happy team that loves your culture! Also, make sure your gestures are genuine.

People have common goals: Everyone wants growth, to have fun, to look clean, to have a nice vehicle, apparel, and technology. When you fulfill what your employees want to take pride in, you create the demand to come and work for you in the industry. Knowing their love languages supports this.

And remember that ROI we talked about? Hiring the right people means they love the culture, too, and they will display this outwardly. An employee might come in with the sweetest motorcycle on the market because they see the pride you take in your trucks, and they want to mirror that through their personal vehicle. They might want to wear all your swag because they feel so good about working for you and want the world to know just how great your company is. When you take pride in your vision and organization, your team will take pride in theirs. That is invaluable advertising.

Culture also includes talking about what's going on in your company outside of your company. The marketing chapter is coming up, but for now, just note that culture means spending money on social media, deciding how your website will look, encouraging Google reviews, etc. All of these elements are interconnected.

Having this culture mindset and using this criteria to build it has enabled me to consistently hire 2.5 people per month since I started my business. I don't put a lot of emotion into it; I just follow the plan.

Let's build your plan now. Read on for my core values examples. If you need to, use a few for inspiration in writing your own.

Examples of Some of My Business's Core Values

1. **Extreme Ownership:** We take complete responsibility for our actions and their consequences.
2. **Being Selfless:** We prioritize the collective good above individual gain.
3. **Always Be Learning:** We foster a culture of continuous growth and improvement.
4. **Leadership Through Action:** We lead by example, taking proactive steps to inspire others.

Your core values should typically contain about four values and include clear explanations of each. You should have them readily accessible during interviews and share them with clients to illustrate your organizational identity and culture.

How to Implement Core Values

Use core values when you have a decision to make. This removes weighing what the right decision is because when someone or something is out of alignment, you will simply follow your core values to correct that person or whatever is out of joint. You will take the emotions out of trying to figure out the right solution. Of course, you will have defined what are fireable offenses, and you will follow protocol and get other departments involved when you need to, but you won't have to sit there and relive your ethics course lessons.

When you are finalizing your core values, make sure you trust them and that you understand why you are applying them to your business. They are critically important as you know by now. Expect to hire and fire off them. Expect to live and die by them. And remember that you need them because you are hiring for the future.

Who you hire will make or break your company.

So, will you hire a thief who steals from you?

Will you hire a go-getter who tries to anticipate what you need?

Will you hire someone who feeds off office gossip to the detriment of the rest of the crew?

Will you hire a right-hand person possessing the enthusiasm and the smarts to become a true leader in your organization?

It is imperative that your foundation is built on core values. Your core values are a direct reflection of your employees—when these align, it is powerful for both parties.

Keep all of these points in mind when it's time to create your own.

Crafting Your Mission Statement

A mission statement is more than just a collection of words; it's a formal declaration of your purpose and values. It provides a shared vision for stakeholders, employees, and clients to rally behind. One of our mission statements is "Building exceptional relationships through exceptional service!" As you can see, it reads a little like a slogan, but it contains a deeper meaning.

Your mission statement should include your purpose and core values and serve as a guiding mantra for your venture. It ensures that everyone involved understands, stands by, and believes in the mission and values, and that they are proud of where they work.

Core Values and Mission Statement Challenge

It's your turn to take some time and write out your core values and mission statement. You don't have to do this now, but you do need to do it before you launch your business. These are your ethical building blocks, so don't skip this exercise!

6

⚜

Creating a Dynamic Business Plan

"Don't make hope your business plan. It's not enough to want it. You have to work it!"

—Mary Christensen

A BUSINESS PLAN is a comprehensive document that captures the essence of your entrepreneurial vision and is necessary to operate for a long time. It outlines your goals, strategies, and action steps, giving life to your business idea.

Consider it a guiding light telling you where to go, empowering you to overcome challenges and succeed.

If you have never written a business plan, don't worry. In this chapter, I'll tell you what a business plan is, why it matters, and how to create one.

I like to think of the business plan as the map of your vision.

Let's say there are two different ways to get from Massachusetts to New York. You can take detours and eventually arrive, or you can take the most direct route and get there quicker, without obstacles turning you around every few miles. Obviously, you want to get there as fast as possible and most efficiently.

A business plan is a living document that will forever be reviewed and changed. Nothing is perfect; life and plans simply change—just like business and your business plan. Learn to accept that early on, and you will be ahead of where I started! Update your business plan as needed as you grow and evolve as a business owner.

Now, let's not procrastinate. Write your plan quickly; get it out there, and know you can always revise it. Your plan doesn't need to be perfect. It just needs to be written.

What Are the Purposes of a Business Plan?

1. It provides a roadmap to achieve your goals and keep you focused on your vision.
2. It communicates your business idea, strategies, and potential to investors, partners, and stakeholders, inspiring confidence and trust.
3. It helps secure funding by proving you are a good risk for potential investors and explains why you are profitable.
4. It helps you identify and mitigate risks, increasing your chances of success.

Unleashing the Forces Behind Business Planning

You need a business plan to help you navigate your business. Its clear direction trickles down into your everyday practices to take you to your planned destination.

We've talked a lot about having a vision and making sure you stick to it to stay in alignment. Your business plan will help you do that. This is the final piece that ties your core values and mission statement together. You are writing down your intentions and visions and breaking down the steps to get to those destinations. With a good strategy, you can also avoid and better handle obstacles without slipping.

A well-written business plan allows you to articulate your unique value proposition. Not only will potential investors understand what you're working with, but everyone will see that you understand business as a whole.

Another great reason to have a plan is that you can customize a version for your employees. I called that a "painted vision."

I have a painted vision on the wall of my office. You can see it when you walk in the door, and every interviewee receives a copy of it when they sit down with our team. It lets us showcase where we want to go financially with the company over the next five years so others can see our potential growth. Your business plan is one part of building a team and company culture. It allows you to own your decisions and steps as you figure out how to overcome obstacles using what you've plotted out in the plan.

Include the following in your business plan:

1. The cheat sheet on how to create a successful employee. (I will provide you with more on this later in the book.)
2. How it will help you hire for the future.
3. How it will help you to always be prospecting.
4. Correct and detailed job descriptions (including using the right tone that will let the prospect decide if they want to be a part of your team. Have this professionally written, if need be).
5. Accountability chart.
6. Org chart.
7. The CRM (customer relationship management) system you use allows you to stay task-oriented and organized within your business; you can manage marketing, customers, invoices, and more. This is the rock in my business. The goal is to always look for your replacement, so you can hire them to grow your business. Having a CRM will help you with this aim and will give you a backbone, enabling a smooth transition for future employees.
8. Applicable funding.
9. Your plans for financial education.
10. Your "painted vision." Remember, you are putting together a leadership plan on where you want to be in five years.

    a. How will you scale?
    b. What's your revenue goal?
    c. How many people do you want on your team?
    d. What are your goals in hiring and building a team?
    e. How will you work your personality to fit with others to be a leader in your business?

The hardest part besides identifying your vision and determining your next steps is extracting your vision and explaining it to your team. It takes a village to build your team, so include that village in your planning.

Using a "painted vision," my team and I built the organization from zero to 60 employees in four years. I want your business plan to reap those same kinds of results.

1. A plan for the employees–to build employee culture.
2. Core values that you can also write on 3x5 cards to share with your prospects (if my interviewees don't take this card when they leave, I don't hire them).

Writing Your Business Plan

First, don't skimp on your research before writing your plan. Thoroughly know your target market, competitors, and customer needs. But don't stop there: Analyze industry trends, customer demographics, and your market dynamic. These critical factors will shape how you write your business plan. Use Google, melissadata.com, and other credible sites to find the most accurate information.

Crystal-clear communication is critical in your business plan, so make your plan easy to understand.

Your business plan should explain the following:

1. Expectations of any partners in the business
2. Your tax model, such as an LLC, Inc., etc. (Consult professionals in areas where needed, such as using a CPA or an attorney, managing a CRM system, and so on.) In addition to consulting these people, ensure that your plan allows you to have the money to pay for

them in the operation of your business—as they will contribute to and even leverage your growth.

3. A section dedicated to ensuring you can pursue financial education. Do not eliminate this, as you are investing in yourself to get to the next level and acquire funding.

Once written and finalized, it's time to leverage the power of your business plan, and that's the best part!

Check out this sample business plan and all the pertinent sections you will want to consider. You can use it as a template when you write your own business plan.

A Sample Business Plan

Business Plan for a $5M Landscaping Company

Investopedia notes a business plan is "A document describing a company's business activities and how it plans to achieve its goals." It also notes, "For startups, a business plan is essential for winning over potential lenders and investors. Established businesses can find one useful for staying on track and not losing sight of their goals." And "There is no single format that a business plan must follow, but there are certain key elements that most companies will want to include."[4]

Before you begin writing, make it easy on yourself: Use bullet points if needed, and back them up with brief, supportive statements.

---

4   Adam Hayes, "Business Plan: What It Is, What's Included, and How to Write One," Investopedia, accessed May 8, 2024, https://www.investopedia. com/terms/b/business-plan.asp.

Remember, our sample business plan concerns a landscaping company in Taunton, Massachusetts.

First, we will write the executive summary.

Executive Summary

1. Note the landscaping company's name, mission, and vision.
2. Highlight the company's commitment to providing exceptional landscaping services that exceed customer expectations through quality workmanship, attention to detail, and personalized experiences.
3. Emphasize the goal of becoming the premier landscaping provider in Taunton, Massachusetts (obviously, you would insert the name of your city and state where your business is located) by building long-term relationships with satisfied customers.

Company Description

1. Provide a detailed overview of the landscaping company, including its legal structure (e.g., LLC), location, and ownership details (include all partners). (Consult a well-versed CPA for financial advice and to better understand why and how to structure your business.)
2. Describe a range of services offered, such as landscape design and installation, lawn maintenance irrigation systems, hardscaping, and seasonal enhancements—as is the case with our sample business. Carve out your niche!
3. Highlight the company's competitive advantage in prioritizing quality service and overall customer service.

Once your executive summary is complete, you can move on to the next sections.

Market Analysis

1. Conduct an in-depth analysis of the local landscaping market in the city, considering factors such as demographics, economic indicators, and industry trends.
2. Identify the target market segment, consisting of homeowners, property management companies, and commercial clients that will value premium landscaping services and are willing to pay for quality and expertise.
3. Analyze the competition, including established landscaping companies in the area, and stress how the company's focus on superior service and customer experience sets it apart.

Marketing and Sales Strategy

1. Develop a comprehensive marketing plan leveraging multiple channels to reach the target market:

    a. Establish a strong brand identity through a professionally designed logo, website, and marketing collateral that convey the company's commitment to quality and customer satisfaction.

    b. Implement targeted online advertising campaigns to increase visibility and attract potential customers searching for landscaping services in the service areas.

    c. Utilize social media platforms, such as Instagram and Facebook, to showcase the company's portfolio, share landscaping tips, and engage with the local community. These actions are undervalued and equal free marketing!

   d. Attend local home and garden shows, distribute flyers, and participate in community events to raise awareness and generate leads.

   e. Develop strategic partnerships with complementary businesses, such as real estate agencies and home builders, to expand the customer base and gain referrals. (Substitute partnerships that will work for your business.)

   f. Prioritize excellent customer service by maintaining open lines of communication, promptly addressing inquiries, and seeking feedback to continuously improve the service experience.

Operations and Organization

1. Outline the organizational structure, including key management positions and responsibilities.

2. Develop a detailed operational plan that covers areas such as hiring and training skilled landscapers, purchasing and maintaining equipment, and sourcing quality materials.

3. Implement efficient scheduling and project management systems to optimize service delivery and ensure on-time completion.

4. Emphasize the company's commitment to employee development through ongoing training programs and certifications.

5. Incorporate sustainable landscaping practices, such as water conservation and eco-friendly materials, to align with the growing demand for environmentally conscious services.

Financial Projections

1. Present a comprehensive financial forecast for the first five years, including projected revenue, expenses, and profitability.
2. Provide a breakdown of startup costs, such as equipment purchases, office setup, and marketing expenditures.
3. Detail ongoing operating expenses, including wages, materials, insurance, and maintenance.
4. Discuss pricing strategies that balance profitability with market competitiveness, considering the target customers' willingness to pay for quality service.
5. Demonstrate a solid understanding of the financial aspects of the business, including cash flow management and strategies for long-term growth and sustainability.

Funding Request

1. Specify the funding required to launch and expand the landscaping company's operations.
2. Justify the funding request by highlighting the potential return on investment, market demand, and competitive advantage.
3. Outline how the funds will be allocated, such as equipment acquisition, marketing campaigns, initial working capital, and professional services (e.g., legal and accounting).

Conclusion

1. Summarize the key elements of the business plan, emphasizing the company's commitment to providing top-tier landscaping services in the service area. It is helpful to include the main overview of each section.
2. Express confidence in the business's potential for success, backed by a thorough market analysis, a solid marketing and sales strategy, efficient operations, and comprehensive financial projections.

Business Plan Challenge

Your next step is to write out a business plan. Don't put a lot of pressure on yourself to make it perfect. Remember what we talked about earlier in this chapter. Your business plan will change over the years that you are operating your business, and due to the changes you will implement and even those outside your control. The goal here is to write down as many details in your business plan as possible. If you like, you can use the sample plan I've included in this chapter to get you started. You can also go to the government's Small Business Administration site: www.sba.gov, and find a template online. Whatever you decide to do, you will be one step further ahead.

7

~≈≈≈≈~

Unlocking Success with Standard Operating Procedures

"Your SOPs are the silent performers in your business, ensuring every task is executed consistently."

—Richard Branson

IN THE WORLD OF BUSINESS, every detail matters. How you handle your operations, interactions with customers, and even the minute tasks behind the scenes all contribute to your success.

Standard operating procedures (SOPs) emerge as your beacon in the fog when pushing for excellence.

In this chapter, we'll dive into what SOPs are, why they are important, and how they can transform your entrepreneurial journey to freedom!

Understanding Standard Operating Procedures

Standard operating procedures, or SOPs for short, are the documented instructions that define how specific tasks, processes, or activities should be carried out within an organization. Think of them as the instruction manual for your business outlining the step-by-step details, responsibilities, and expected outcomes for various operations, ensuring consistency and uniformity.

Any company doing substantial revenue needs to include SOPs in its strategy. Even if you don't think you are making enough money to warrant using them, put them in place, and you will give yourself a leg up as you grow to the size you dream of. This will also make your life easier. Hard work and grit only get you so far. Can anyone off the street come in and do your job? If you want a work-life balance . . . these will be your best friend. SOPs allow you to scale without losing a beat; they are the most efficient way to build yourself out properly.

You will need to communicate well and often with your significant other. Sharing your SOPs will help them understand what you're responsible for and how much time it may take. Inviting the person you love the most into your world might even excite them a little about what you are doing and make them feel closer to you.

Take it from me; there's nothing better than having your family's support. Sharing SOPs is one way to do this.

In addition to taking measures to nurture your personal relationship, life is easier if you document what you do daily, both now and in the future. If I had started this when I first opened my doors, I would have had more quality control.

As you write out your SOPs, accept that what you are building now may not match what you want in 5 or 10 years. That is completely normal, so don't stress out about that fact. Just write down what is pertinent today, and when it's time to change your SOP because your processes have changed, go ahead and do that.

SOPs also make your company more attractive to buyers. That's because new owners can run it without being involved. They can simply set motions into play and enjoy profitability.

Why Do SOPs Matter?

Imagine a world without traffic rules. Wouldn't it be chaos? SOPs serve as the traffic rules for your business. They provide clarity, structure, and a roadmap for your team to navigate operations.

More reasons you don't want to skip documenting your SOPs:

1. **Efficiency and Consistency**: SOPs are the ultimate tools for streamlining processes. They eliminate guesswork and ensure that each task is completed the same way every time. This consistency leads to greater efficiency, fewer errors, and improved quality.
2. **Effective Training**: SOPs are pivotal in employee onboarding and training. New hires can quickly grasp

their responsibilities, and existing team members can refresh their knowledge when needed. This reduces the learning curve and boosts productivity.

3. **Risk Mitigation**: Any industry errors can have severe consequences. SOPs are a shield against potential disasters. They enforce compliance with industry regulations and safety protocols within the office and most industry fields.

4. **Scalability**: This is my favorite point! As your business grows, SOPs become indispensable. They ensure that your processes remain consistent across different locations or teams. This helps with the growth of your team and ensures all systems are followed, no matter how many people are added or how much your input and output changes. But when it changes to the point where processes are affected, it's time to update your SOP.

5. **Quality Control**: Maintaining consistent quality in your products or services is non-negotiable. SOPs outline the best practices to achieve this.

6. **Time and Resource Management**: SOPs eliminate unnecessary steps or redundancies, saving time and resources. With optimized processes, your business becomes more cost-effective and competitive.

7. **Continuous Improvement**: SOPs are not static documents but are living guides that evolve with your business. Regular reviews and updates keep your operations in sync with changing industry trends and technologies.

8. **Customer Experience**: For businesses prioritizing a consistent customer experience, SOPs ensure that every interaction meets the same high standards. Your customers will recognize and appreciate your quality of service.

Don't skip crafting your SOPs—this is a minimal investment, and as you grow, you won't always have the time to dedicate to your SOPs. It might feel a little early in your business game, but you still need to do it.

Crafting Your SOPs

It's crucial to create your SOPs with care and precision to harness their full power. Each SOP should have a clear purpose, process, and measurable outcomes. Start with your business's most critical tasks or processes, and gradually expand your library of SOPs as needed.

You can start crafting your SOPs even when you are the only employee in the company. Doing this prepares you for your first employee so you can save time training and focus on the sales and growth of your company. SOPs can be a live document, a video recording, or any other way of documenting a process that fits within your business. Using SOPs truly differentiates businesses and allows business owners to get back their time. Time is not purchased; it is created!

Ideas to Record/Create Your SOPs

You don't need 200 pages to document your SOPs; don't overcomplicate the matter. Consider doing the following:

1. Video and screen record yourself talking about every process in your business.
2. Write your SOPs off the recording.
3. These two pieces will correlate with each other.

As you start your entrepreneurial journey and develop your company's processes, try to avoid backtracking your progress. Breaking down your methods enables you to start buying back your time and grow the right way.

8

The Power of
Marketing

"The best marketing doesn't feel like marketing."
—Tom Fishburne

MARKETING IS MANDATORY.

In today's competitive business landscape, marketing isn't just a strategy; it's necessary for thriving and expanding your business. Marketing serves as the lifeblood of your company, connecting you with your target audience, building brand awareness so people will learn who you are and what you can provide as a service to them, and ultimately driving revenue.

Imagine that your company is as successful as Kleenex. This brand's name has replaced the word "tissue," a generic term. That's killer branding! People everywhere refer to using Kleenex all the time; it doesn't even occur to them to think of a different term. What if that was your goal—to have your company name coming out of every mouth worldwide? Hey, Kleenex did it. Why not you?

What about the McDonald's Happy Meal? This menu item was a game-changer, combining a child-friendly meal with an enticing toy. McDonald's strategic move tapped into the desires of both children and parents, creating a unique offering that set the restaurant apart from its competitors.

By bundling food and toys together, McDonald's not only increased its appeal to children, but it also created a compelling reason for parents to choose their restaurant over others.

The Happy Meal became an instant hit, driving customer loyalty, boosting sales, and establishing McDonald's as a family-friendly brand. It demonstrated the power of understanding customer needs, crafting an innovative concept, and leveraging the emotional connection between children and toys to drive business growth.

I bring this up because there are different levels of branding and marketing.

In this chapter, we'll explore the basics of marketing (that will give you the jump on that Kleenex dream) and why it's not only lucrative but essential for your business's success. We'll also jump into the world of social media marketing and highlight the opportunities these platforms offer, all at your fingertips and without breaking the bank.

You are going to hear two terms as you read through this chapter: "marketing" and "branding." They might sound like they cover the same category, but they have very different meanings.

Marketing is the art and science of telling your story; it is the strategy that showcases your offerings that ultimately engages with potential customers. It is behind the scenes of advertising, the star of the show, the customer-facing identity people see.

Branding goes beyond a logo or a tagline; it represents the emotional connection between your business and your audience. That connection is important because when people attach to you and your product, they want to work with you. Branding builds trust to help influence customer decisions.

Here are a few other compelling reasons why your marketing and branding are crucial for your business:

1. **Invaluable ROIs**: There are so many variables to ROIs, and when done right, they all feed into and enhance each other.
2. **Building Brand Awareness**: Effective marketing efforts introduce your brand to the world. It involves creating a recognizable name and identity that sticks in people's minds. This familiarity encourages trust and makes customers more likely to choose your products or services over competitors.
3. **Connecting with Your Audience**: Marketing helps you identify and connect with your target audience. You can tailor your marketing campaigns to speak directly to them by understanding their needs, preferences, and pain points. This personal touch builds stronger relationships with your customers.

4. **Generating Leads and Sales:** This is the most important point. There is no company without sales. Marketing generates leads, turning potential customers into paying ones. Through various marketing channels, you can attract individuals interested in what you offer, guiding them through the buyer's journey and, eventually, converting them into loyal customers.

5. **Staying Competitive:** In a world of fierce competition, businesses that don't market themselves effectively risk falling behind. Marketing keeps you in the game, helping you stay competitive and relevant in your industry.

How to Get Started with Marketing

Now that you understand the importance of marketing, you might wonder how to get started. Here are some steps to begin your marketing journey:

1. **Define Your Target Audience:** Identify your ideal customers—those most likely to benefit from your products or services. You can consider demographic and psychographic information to define your audience. Your audience may also be comprised of multiple segments: different types of clients that you want to work with and whose pain points you will solve.

2. **Craft a Unique Value Proposition:** Determine what sets your business apart from the competition. In other words, why should customers choose you?

3. **Set Clear Marketing Goals:** What do you want to achieve with your marketing efforts? Establish specific goals, whether brand awareness, lead generation, or sales.

4. **Choose the Right Marketing Channels:** Depending on your audience and goals, select the appropriate marketing channels. This might include social media, email marketing, content marketing, or paid advertising. It will likely include multiple channels deploying at the same time to maximize your marketing efforts. It's crucial to utilize various marketing channels, both on and offline, to reach a diverse audience. Different customers have different preferences when it comes to communication channels. By diversifying your marketing efforts, you increase your chances of reaching a broader audience and capturing their attention. Utilize any relevant channels to expand your reach. We incorporate organic Facebook marketing along with paid marketing.

5. **Create Engaging and Consistent Content:** Develop high-quality, relevant content that resonates with your audience. This could be blog posts, videos, infographics, or social media updates. Consistency in messaging is vital for effective marketing. Ensure your brand message remains consistent across all channels to create a cohesive and recognizable brand image. This consistent messaging helps build trust and familiarity with your audience, making it easier for them to connect with your business.

6. **Analyze and Adjust:** Use data and analytics to measure the effectiveness of your marketing campaigns. Track and analyze your performance. Use your platforms' analytics options or third-party tools to monitor metrics like reach, engagement, click-through rates, and conversions. This data will help you understand what's working and what needs adjustment, enabling you to refine your social media strategy over time. Don't worry; imperfect action is better than no action at all.

I don't expect you to be a professional marketer, but over time, you will master your craft. Always adjust your strategies based on what works best for your business and perform tests to assess where changes need to be made to improve metrics. There are many great tools available for marketing, such as email marketing, text automation and using AI. But keep in mind that this new addition to technology is not a catch-all. AI is a gatherer of pre-existing content in the marketplace written by someone else. AI mashes up what it finds and regurgitates it for your use. It is not good at sounding human. It doesn't check whether the content is true or credible, and sometimes, it is redundant. Ensure you review what it generates, and check it for accuracy, etc.

Social Media Marketing: The Game Changer

Now, let's talk about the digital revolution of social media and the incredible opportunities it presents for your marketing efforts. Social media platforms like Facebook, Instagram, TikTok, X, and LinkedIn have transformed how businesses reach and engage with audiences.

In particular, Facebook and Instagram are two powerhouses that you shouldn't underestimate and that can provide mega visibility to your business. As you experiment and learn through social media, plan for algorithms to be forever changing and to keep up with the new rules governing visibility and how many people will be exposed to your brand. This is how you will grow your business and network.

The more people you know, the more you will grow—the more people will know, like, and trust you.

As you advertise, don't *sell* your business to people. Stay relevant and top-of-mind; build partnerships and relationships. When I started, I had 100 local friends; now, I have 5,000 friends worldwide. So, when I say growth is possible and even probable when you use social media consistently, I mean it. I'm living it.

FYI, a smaller follower of more engaged people is always more valuable than a larger following of people who might not even know what you do or anything about your business.

Facebook (Meta): The Social Giant

Google tells me that there are approximately three billion monthly active users on Facebook. It is a colossal platform that allows businesses to:

1. **Create Business Pages**: Establish a professional online presence for your brand, complete with essential information, contact details, and a feed to showcase your products or services.
2. **Run Targeted Ads**: Facebook's ad platform lets you precisely target your ideal customers based on demographics, interests, and behaviors. This means your ads reach people most likely to engage with your brand.
3. **Interact with Customers**: Use Facebook to chat with your audience through posts, comments, and direct messages. Customer feedback and engagement help you refine your offerings and build trust.

Instagram: Visual Storytelling

With its emphasis on visual content, Instagram is perfect for showcasing your brand's personality and creativity. Here's why it's an essential marketing tool:

1. **Visual Appeal:** Instagram's focus on photos and videos enables you to visually represent your brand, products, and services in a compelling way.
2. **Hashtags and Discoverability:** The strategic use of hashtags makes your content discoverable by users interested in topics related to your business, significantly expanding your reach.
3. **Engagement and Authenticity:** Instagram's interactive features, such as Reels, allow you to engage with your audience authentically. Show behind-the-scenes glimpses of your business, share customer stories, and foster community.

I highly suggest you learn more about marketing as you continue your business journey. It's an ever-evolving field. To continue learning and improving your marketing skills, consider looking into online courses, books, blogs, and masterminds.

Remember, marketing is a journey. Embrace the process, adapt to changes, and watch your business flourish as you connect with your audience and drive growth through effective marketing strategies.

Always keep in mind that customers do business with people they know, like, and trust. They want to be able to relate to you and know that you are essentially the same. You have struggles; they have struggles. You have wins; they have wins. We are all more alike than we think.

Marketing Challenge

When you are writing out your posts on social media, keep the 80/20 rule in mind that says the majority of what you will share on your personal social media pages should be geared toward lifestyle posts, like what you and your family are up to, pictures of events in your life, inspiring content you would like to post, and other personal details. Twenty percent of your content can revolve around business or asking for the sale. You want to do this to ensure that your page isn't overloaded with sales-y content that will turn off your followers. This is more of a soft-sell approach, and it can work wonders in creating affinity for you and, eventually, your company.

The 80/20 rule is a general strategy that may or may not work for you. My job is to present you with options, and your job is to find what works for you. Every business is different, so keep that in mind as you try out the suggestions in this book. I am giving you the tactics that worked for me. You might have to make adjustments when you implement recommendations—and that is just fine. The goal is whatever works for you.

9

On the Runway:
Taking Flight

"You only fail if you quit."

—Unknown

OUR JOURNEY TOGETHER IS NEARING ITS END, and it's time to be selfish and take time for you. It's time to embrace your passion and let it drive you. The information in these pages has equipped you with the tools, wisdom, and courage to step into the entrepreneurial world. I can't wait for you to take that leap and see how high you can go.

A Few Final Thoughts

Align your actions with your vision.

Dreams won't work without moving forward.

Once you put this book down, promise yourself that you will work hard and put in the effort. Show your friends, family, and community what you are about to create.

If you are working for someone else, don't give up on your dreams and think this is the end of owning and operating your own business. Companies need intrapreneurs. The tools I've provided can help you transition out of your job and into full-time entrepreneurship. However, this may not be your path.

Entrepreneurship is a wild ride, but I wouldn't want it any other way. I'm betting once you get a real taste of it, you will agree.

Commit to constantly educating yourself so you can last in your field. Reading this book and others like it is one way to do that, and it's important to continually gather new information.

Use the right tools for the right job—like the ones in this book and others you haven't heard of yet. Learn about them by engaging in virtual partnerships, researching YouTube videos, and taking advantage of other resources, trainings, working with mentors, etc.

Reach for heights you never thought possible. Follow your heart and make quick, confident decisions. No one ever plans to be an Apple. Jeff Bezos probably astounded himself with his success. He started Amazon out of his garage in 1994, and in 1997, he finally gained traction.

I remember Amazon exploding into the beast it is today. Learn from his story. Don't discount yourself, and give yourself as many tools as possible.

If after reading this book and doing a little exploring of your passions and interests, you discover you don't want his dream, that's okay, too.

The most important takeaway from this book is to go after the dream you want.

That's a lot to bite off, isn't it? It would be hard enough for a person coming from an ideal childhood.

I know it can feel impossible when you've come from trying circumstances. Sometimes, we might feel so beaten down and invisible that all we want to do is shut ourselves away forever. I felt like that. Maybe you have, too. It helped me to remember that everyone has tragedy and trauma in their childhoods.

One day, after mastering your mindset training, I promise you won't let your past define you. You won't let it limit you. That will be the greatest day of your life—when you see what you have been through for what it is—a way to travel to a stronger position in life. I encourage you to build your resilience to fight back against what wants to hold you down.

Now, a last warning before you close this book: entrepreneurship won't be easy, and if you want to work 40 hours a week, this isn't your gig. Some people think because you work for yourself, you can work less than a standard full-time workweek—sure if you want to go belly up. Knock yourself out. To achieve at the levels you envy others operating at, you will need to be nearly obsessed.

Even if entrepreneurship is for you, it will be exhausting. You will experience failures, wins, and losses. Use these failures as priceless lessons you can't learn anywhere else but through experience. Failures tell us exactly what road not to take—resulting in a lot of saved time and frustration. Failures lead to success.

Be coachable . . . This is so important. If you keep at it and overcome what is thrown at you personally and professionally, you will flourish.

Whatever your future holds, the experiences shared in this book can be applied to any endeavor in your business and life. There's no reason you can't do what other people are doing—whether you are planning to fulfill your dream or be inspired by theirs. I know you can do it. You finished this book, which proves you have what it takes. I know you picked it up because you want to change your life. Besides, you already have the best tool that can work anytime, anywhere, and under any circumstance: your belief in yourself.

When the day comes that you reach your dreams under your own power, do me a favor and reflect for a minute on all the work you've done.

Tell yourself you're not lucky; you're unstoppable. There's a big difference.

Knowledge Recap

USE TOOLS LIKE MASTERMINDS OR SOCIAL MEDIA GROUPS in your entrepreneurial journey. Follow those who inspire you and/or who you can relate to. Do extra things like setting alarms for actions that will push you forward daily, and return to this book as many times as you need to throughout your career to grow, rise to the next level, or regroup.

1. Revisit the Visionary and Integrator Test. Confirm it still aligns with your goals: rocketfueluniversity.com/quiz/crystallizer-quiz-hs-norandom-privateapp.php
2. Check out 75 Hard or other resilience programs to build up mentally and physically.
3. Define your vision statement. Refer to the end of Chapter 4 for the specific information you need to complete it.

Alright, it's time to fly.

This is YOUR story.

Go live it.

Be resilient.

More importantly, be YOU.

Recommended Books

1. *Good to Great*, by Jim Collins
2. *Traction*, by Gino Wickman
3. *Extreme Ownership*, by Jocko Willink and Leif Babin
4. *Rich Dad Poor Dad*, by Robert Kiyosaki and Sharon Lechter

About the Author

MARC MASON primarily grew up in East Taunton, Massachusetts, which many would describe as the country portion of a city. He graduated from a vocational high school plumbing program as the first in its history to obtain his master plumbing license where he learned the skills that allowed him to later establish his first small business. Now, as the owner of multiple businesses, he finds balance in his home with his beautiful wife and his favorite job title . . . Daddy.

Disclaimer

THIS BOOK IS A TRUTHFUL RECOLLECTION OF ACTUAL EVENTS IN THE AUTHOR'S LIFE. The events, places, and conversations in this book have been recreated from memory. The names and details of some individuals or entities have been changed to respect their privacy.

The information provided within this book is for general informational, educational, and entertainment purposes only. The author and publisher are not offering such information as business, investment or legal advice, or any other kind of professional advice, and the advice and ideas contained herein may not be suitable for your situation.

Any use of the information provided within this book is at your own risk, and it is provided without any express or implied warranties or guarantees on the part of the author or publisher. No warranty may be created or extended by sales representatives or written sales materials. You should seek the services of a competent professional before beginning any business endeavor or investment.

Neither the author nor the publisher shall be held liable or responsible to any person or entity with respect to any financial, commercial, or other loss or damages (including but not limited to special, incidental, or consequential damages) caused or alleged to have been caused, directly or indirectly, by the use of any of the information contained herein.